"This is a book primarily about J[...] is reflected in the subtitle *Listen.*[...] Jones guides us in listening to the prayers of Jesus for what they tell us about Jesus, and then what they tell us about prayer. Think of it as a Christology viewed through the lens of Jesus's prayers. Jones's purpose is much deeper than just drawing principles of prayer from the prayers of Jesus; he takes us into a deeper understanding of who Jesus is and what he has done for us, and then applies that to the prayer life of the believer in Christ."

Donald S. Whitney, Associate Dean of the School of Theology and Professor of Biblical Spirituality, The Southern Baptist Theological Seminary; author, *Spiritual Disciplines for the Christian Life* and *Praying the Bible*

"Mark Jones has done it again. He distills the beauty, majesty, and mystery of Jesus into accessible and transformative food for the soul. No other writer today says so much about Christ in such profound, readable, provocative, and rich ways. The humanity, vulnerability, authority, and glory of our Lord jump out of every page. Read this book."

Dan MacDonald, Senior Pastor, Grace Toronto Church

"What a wonderful idea—to access the person and work of our Savior through his prayers. The result is a beautiful and soul-satisfying book that will not only teach you more about Jesus but also teach you how to pray. If your soul is dry and your prayers are dead, here is living water to revive and refresh you."

David Murray, Professor of Old Testament and Practical Theology, Puritan Reformed Theological Seminary

"In offering us a profoundly theological explanation of why our great God and Savior Jesus Christ needed to pray to his Father in the power of the Holy Spirit, Mark Jones gives us inspiration to do the same. With the assistance of some of the great Puritans of the past, and often poignantly written, *The Prayers of Jesus* is a bold and biblical exploration of this much-neglected topic."

Lee Gatiss, Director, Church Society; author, *The Forgotten Cross*

"Christians with an appetite for knowing Jesus will find a feast in *The Prayers of Jesus*. Mark Jones serves up the finest in devotional food, teaching us how to come to the Father by observing the prayer life of his Son. I heartily commend not only the bite-size chapters but also Jones's meaty historical and theological introduction."

Chad Van Dixhoorn, Professor of Church History, Westminster Theological Seminary

"Few living voices have proved as trustworthy on Christology as Mark Jones. And appropriately, Jones is not just a scholar but also a pastor. Watch as the nuance and care of a scholar's treatment of Christology takes on the heart and practical concerns of a pastor. As heaven kissed earth in the incarnation, so here Christology forms and fills the everyday life of faith, as we learn the most basic and beautiful of devotional acts from the Master, who is both holy God and fellow man. I'm not aware of another book quite like this remarkable study."

David Mathis, Executive Editor, desiringGod.org; Pastor, Cities Church, Minneapolis/St. Paul; author, *Habits of Grace*

"Prayer, it has been said, reveals the truth of who we are. The prayers of Jesus, then, allow us to clearly see our Lord for who he truly is. From beginning to end, this is a book about Jesus. And so, for the Christian reader, this is also a delightful book—one in which every page invites us to know Christ more intimately. Read and be blessed."

Megan Hill, author, *Praying Together* and *Contentment*; Editor, The Gospel Coalition

The Prayers of Jesus

The Prayers of Jesus

Listening to and Learning
from Our Savior

Mark Jones

WHEATON, ILLINOIS

The Prayers of Jesus: Listening to and Learning from Our Savior

Copyright © 2019 by Mark Jones

Published by Crossway
                1300 Crescent Street
                Wheaton, Illinois 60187

Cover design: Jorge Canedo Estrada

First printing 2019

Printed in the United States of America

Trade paperback ISBN: 978-1-4335-6281-5
ePub ISBN: 978-1-4335-6284-6
PDF ISBN: 978-1-4335-6282-2
Mobipocket ISBN: 978-1-4335-6283-9

Library of Congress Cataloging-in-Publication Data

Names: Jones, Mark, 1980– author.
Title: The prayers of Jesus: listening to and learning from our Savior / Mark Jones.
Description: Wheaton, Illinois: Crossway, [2019] | Includes bibliographical references and index.
Identifiers: LCCN 2018030460 (print) | LCCN 2018050887 (ebook) | ISBN 9781433562822 (pdf) | ISBN 9781433562839 (mobi) | ISBN 9781433562846 (epub) | ISBN 9781433562815 (tp)
Subjects: LCSH: Jesus Christ—Prayers. | Prayer—Christianity.
Classification: LCC BV229 (ebook) | LCC BV229 .J655 2019 (print) | DDC 232.9/5—dc23
LC record available at https://lccn.loc.gov/2018030460

Crossway is a publishing ministry of Good News Publishers.

VP		29	28	27	26	25	24	23	22	21	20	19
15	14	13	12	11	10	9	8	7	6	5	4	3	2	1

To

Barb Jones, Garry Vanderveen, Delores Vandeyar,
Steven Wedgeworth, Leigh Robinson, Jonathan Tomes,
Alicia Du, Jack Chen, and Alda Craukamp,

with appreciation for help offered
during the writing of this book

Contents

Acknowledgments 13

Introducing Our Praying Lord 15

1 Jesus Prayed from His Mother's Breasts 27
  PSALM 22:9–10

2 Jesus Prayed "Abba! Father" 37
  JOHN 17:1

3 Jesus Prayed in Secret 43
  LUKE 5:16

4 Jesus Prayed the Lord's Prayer 51
  MATTHEW 6:9–13

5 Jesus Prayed Joyfully in the Spirit 61
  LUKE 10:21

6 Jesus Prayed Knowing He Would Be Heard 67
  JOHN 11:41–42

7 Jesus Prayed for His Father's Glory 73
  JOHN 12:27–28

8 Jesus Prayed for His Own Glory 79
  JOHN 17:1

9   Jesus Prayed concerning Eternal Life 85
    JOHN 17:1–2

10 Jesus Prayed for Us to Know God and Himself 91
    JOHN 17:3

11 Jesus Prayed for the Glory He Had Before the World
    Existed 99
    JOHN 17:4–5

12 Jesus Prayed concerning God's Self-Disclosure 107
    JOHN 17:6–8

13 Jesus Prayed for the Elect to Glorify Him 113
    JOHN 17:9–10

14 Jesus Prayed That the Father Would Protect the
    Church...119
    JOHN 17:11–12

15 Jesus Prayed for His Disciples to Be Joyful 125
    JOHN 17:13

16 Jesus Prayed for His Disciples in the World 131
    JOHN 17:14–16

17 Jesus Prayed for His Disciples to Be Sanctified 137
    JOHN 17:17–19

18 Jesus Prayed for Church Unity 143
    JOHN 17:20–21

19 Jesus Prayed for Us to Receive His Glory 153
    JOHN 17:22–23

20 Jesus Prayed for His People to Be with Him 161
    JOHN 17:24

21 Jesus Prayed with Confidence 167
    JOHN 17:25–26

22 Jesus Prayed in Great Distress 173
    MARK 14:32–34

23 Jesus Prayed for Deliverance 179
    MARK 14:35–36

24 Jesus Prayed for His Enemies 187
    LUKE 23:34

25 Jesus Prayed with a Loud Cry 193
    MARK 15:34

26 Jesus Prayed His Final Prayer 199
    LUKE 23:46

Notes 205

General Index 211

Scripture Index 217

Acknowledgments

I would like to thank Crossway for continuing to be a great publisher to work with. They always exceed my expectations, and their diligence and hard work, on so many fronts, is deeply appreciated.

I would like to thank Dr. Bob McKelvey for reading through the entire manuscript of this book and offering many suggestions. I am privileged to have such a gifted friend.

Many thanks to Jorge Canedo Estrada, who continues to design wonderful book covers for me (and also serve wonderfully in the church where I minister).

Also, I could not write books if it were not for the support of my local church: Faith Vancouver/Surrey Presbyterian Church.

My family also continues to show great patience with me when I get into my reading, researching, and writing groove.

A special thank you to Todd Stanton at St. John's Park Baptist Church in Sydney, Australia, for inviting my family and me down to do a conference on the topic of the prayers of Jesus in August 2018.

Finally, to the readers of this book, thank you for taking the time to read my work. I hope and pray the book will bless your soul and do you much spiritual good as you seek to listen to and learn from the Savior, Jesus Christ.

Introducing Our Praying Lord

As an author and pastor, I wouldn't want to scare off my readers with an introduction that is more difficult than the rest of the book. We have so much to learn from the prayer life of Jesus. However, understanding and appreciating our praying Lord necessitates knowing him through a good theology of Christ (Christology). Even the word *Christology* can be frightening, but it is really just the study of Christ's person and his work. So, if you can stay with me through this introduction, I believe it will be helpful for understanding the prayers of Jesus. But if you find its language a bit too technical, reading it isn't absolutely necessary for you to enjoy (and learn from) this book.

All Christians have a Christology. But can your understanding of Christ's person do justice to his prayer life so that his "loud cries and tears" (Heb. 5:7) to his Father, whom he revered with godly fear, were real and not somehow pretended?

Since the early church, theologians, even some of the greatest names known to us, have struggled to offer a meaningful account of the prayer life of Jesus of Nazareth. In a penetrating study on the Christology of Cyril of Alexandria and Nestorius, John Anthony McGuckin suggests, "Cyril would explain Jesus' prayer life as an economic exercise done largely for our instruction and edification."[1]

Did Jesus, who is of the same essence with God, pray basically as an example for those who observed him? Or did Jesus, who is also of the same essence with man (possessing body and soul), pray because he needed to pray for his own sake as well as ours? If the latter, which I believe is the case, what does it mean for us to say he "needed" to pray? These are important questions, and they bring us to the heart of our Christology.

If Jesus did not pray out of necessity, then something has gone wrong with our understanding of who he is. A close examination of the references to Christ's prayers, as well as the implications of his teaching ministry, reveals that his prayers were at the heart of his obedient and dependent life before the Father. In the face of temptation and trial, Jesus sought God, believing that God could and would help him in his time of need. But how can we speak of the "need" of One who is not just fully man but also God?

Interpreting Chalcedon

The Westminster Shorter Catechism (Q. 21) provides a valuable summary statement concerning Christ's person: "The only Redeemer of God's elect is the Lord Jesus Christ [John 14:6], who, being the eternal Son of God [Ps. 2:7], became man [Isa. 9:6], and so was, and continues to be, God and man in two distinct natures, and one person, forever [Acts 1:11]."

Not only does this answer ring true; there is nothing in this statement that an orthodox Christian would deny. Yet statements concerning Christ's person (one person, two natures), even among orthodox thinkers, were historically not quite so simple. Theological conflicts prompted the Council of Chalcedon (451 AD), which resulted in the (beautifully written) Chalcedonian Creed. Some believe that Chalcedon resolved the question about what it means to affirm an orthodox view of

Christ's person. In general, this is true. But that does not mean the story is complete or fully resolved.

Not surprisingly, the two major sides in the debate, namely, the Alexandrian and Antiochene schools, may not have been fully satisfied with the outcome of Chalcedon. Who actually "won" is still disputed. Some acknowledge that both Alexandrian and Antiochene emphases can be found in the document. The Alexandrians (i.e., "the Cyrilline party") emphasized the unity of the person and his divinity, whereas the Antiochenes focused on the distinction between the two natures, aiming especially to offer a fully human Jesus. The danger of the Alexandrian position was that it could lean toward the heresy of Eutyches, whose view of Christ threatened the integrity of the two natures because of an undue emphasis on the divine nature at the expense of the human nature. On the other hand, the danger of the Antiochene position was to lean toward the heresy of Nestorianism, a view of Christ that threatened the unity of Christ's person because of an undue separation of the natures.

The matter only becomes more complicated when one considers that Nestorius, for the sake of unity, was willing to affirm that Mary was, as Cyril had strenuously affirmed, *theotokos* ("the Mother of God"; lit. "God-bearer"), though some question his integrity in this "confession." Additionally, it remains questionable whether his own theology threatened the union of human and divine natures in Christ. In other words, he had a heresy named after him that he likely did not espouse. Furthermore, Cyril sometimes makes statements that seem more Antiochene than Alexandrian. Whatever the case in this historical drama, the creed and later Reformed confessions and catechisms affirm that there are two natures in one person. The more pressing question focuses on how these two natures relate to each other in the one person.

Western Trajectories

Leaving aside the Christology of the Eastern church—a valuable and important study in its own right—the Western church has always made a distinction between the two otherwise inseparable natures of Christ, who is of the same substance with both humanity and God. But traditions in the Western church understood the relation of these two natures somewhat differently. For example, Roman Catholic theologians generally came to the conclusion that because of the hypostatic union, Christ possessed from birth the beatific vision of God; that is, Christ walked not by faith but by sight. His human nature received all the gifts that were ever to be given to him at the moment of his incarnation. The Lutherans went in a different, more extreme, direction. They agreed with the Roman Catholic theologians that Christ received a communication of graces all at once at the incarnation. However, they also maintained that Christ also received a communication of divine attributes to the human nature at the incarnation.

Perhaps the most sophisticated version of the Lutheran model posits that the communication of attributes is unidirectional, that is, the divine attributes are communicated to the human nature and not the other way. Even so, both Roman Catholic and Lutheran theologians elevate the human nature above the boundaries set for it in Christ's life of humiliation. In this way, they cannot adequately account for development in Christ's human nature. In fact, the reality of Christ's state of humiliation comes into question: Did Christ really need to learn and be taught (Isa. 50:4)?

Moreover, one has to wonder what type of prayer life Christ had according to the Christology of those Lutherans and Roman Catholics who elevate his human nature to the degree that they do. Did Christ receive help from God in his time of need when he prayed?

Opposition to Roman Catholic and Lutheran Christology by Reformed theologians can be explained by their emphasis that "the finite is not capable of the infinite." In response to Lutheran claims, this maxim emphasizes that the finite humanity of Christ was and (still) is not capable of receiving infinite attributes (e.g., omnipresence and omniscience). Thus, Christ's human nature, which includes both his body and soul, experiences limitations. This remains true even though his human and divine natures are hypostatically united. Indeed, even in his state of exaltation, Christ's glorified human nature remains distinct from his divine nature and cannot attain to or fully comprehend the divine. If it could, he would not really still be the God-*man*.

The relationship between the two natures in the one person is voluntary. The divine nature does not necessarily "engulf" the human nature, obliterating it to the mere appearance of flesh. All communications between the divine and human natures in Christ are voluntary, so that if he confesses a type of ignorance (see Mark 13:32) according to the limitations of his human nature, it is because we need to keep in mind that the divine nature does not *necessarily* reveal to his human nature all things (which is impossible). A voluntary relation between the two natures in the one person protects the integrity of Christ's human nature so that his own prayers are really those of a man who needs to pray for the sake of his soul.

Reformed Christology

Reformed theologians insisted upon the integrity of the two natures of Christ because, as noted above, the essence of the godhead is incommunicable. So, even though Christ was a perfect man—the visible image of the invisible God—his human nature remains finite. Critics of Reformed Christology have understood this view as borderline Nestorian, and so it was vitally important for Reformed theologians to maintain that Christ's two natures are united in a single person. Therefore, the Son of God assumed a human nature and not a human person. This *anhypostatic* (impersonal) assumption suggests that the human nature subsists only in the person of the Logos. Christ's human nature is *enhypostatic*, that is, becomes personal ("identified") at the moment of the incarnation when the Logos assumed a human nature. In other words, the human nature exists in and is thereby "personalized" (hypostatized) by the Logos. This is why we do not speak of natures doing things, but rather the *person* acting according to each nature.

The Alexandrian theologians, particularly Cyril, maintained that the identity of the person is the Logos. Thus, for Cyril, the Logos acts as the agent of all that is done in the human nature, a position that potentially raises a host of problems. The potential problem with this model has to do with how the integrity of the human nature is preserved. In other words, how can we speak of truly human experiences? Moreover, ascribing suffering to the Logos while affirming divine impassibility proves to be incoherent. Consequently, many Reformed theologians have used the idea of "person" to refer to Christ in his two natures and not the Logos simpliciter (plainly/simply). The incarnation constituted a "complex" (or, "composite") person, which reflects the two natures of the God-man, Jesus Christ.

Following from this view of Christ's person, many Reformed theologians have spoken of the "communication of properties," which also includes the "communication of operations," since the phrases taken together reflect the person doing the work. The Westminster Confession of Faith describes these concepts in the following manner: "Christ, in the work of mediation, acts according to both natures, by each nature doing that which is proper to itself; yet, by reason of the unity of the person, that which is proper to one nature is sometimes in Scripture attributed to the person denominated by the other nature" (WCF, 8.7).

The "person" does not act through his human nature as his instrument; rather, the God-man acts according to both natures. This point of doctrine was actually a source of contention between the Reformed orthodox and various Roman Catholic writers who held that Christ performed his acts of mediation only as man.

Roman Catholic theologians, such as Robert Bellarmine, argued that Christ is Mediator not according to his divine nature but only in his human nature. Reformed theologians argued that if only Christ's human nature mediated, then another human could mediate with equal efficacy before and after the incarnation. By anchoring the natures of Christ in the unity of the person, Reformed theologians refused to speak of Christ's mediatorial work as simply the work of a human. No, Christ's mediatorial work was the work of the God-man, Jesus Christ.

Bellarmine also reasoned that if Christ mediated according to his divine nature, then the Father and the Spirit would also be Mediators. In response, Reformed theologians argued that this type of reasoning would lead to the conclusion that since the Son was made flesh, then also the Father and the Spirit were made flesh. There is essence-appropriate language: all three persons share the same divine attributes because they are all

God. But there is also persons-appropriate language: the Father is not begotten, but the Son is begotten. The Spirit proceeds from the Father and the Son, but the Father does not proceed from the Spirit, and so forth. Personal properties may differ among a shared divine essence.

Affirming that Christ mediates according to both natures as one person enables us to understand a passage such as Acts 20:28, which speaks of the church being purchased by the blood of God. Based on the communication of properties and operations, Reformed theologians had no problem saying that God died—even though it was impossible for Christ's divine nature to suffer or die—because his work is attributed to the whole person. The whole Christ is God and man because this speaks of the person, but the whole *of* Christ is not God and man because a distinction between the two natures must be maintained.[2] So, may we sing that glorious hymn "And Can It Be?," especially the words "how can it be that thou, my God, shouldst die for me?" Based on the doctrine of the communication of properties, the answer is yes!

The above shows that Reformed Christology had its own distinctive emphases when compared with Catholic and Lutheran accounts of the person of Christ. Most readers would find nothing too controversial in the account above. However, in the Puritan tradition, for example, one finds a somewhat unique and distinctive emphasis on the role of the Spirit in relation to the person of Christ in order to bring coherence to the relations between the two natures of Christ.

The Christological Role of the Spirit

Most Christians assume that Christ was able to perform miracles because he was God. That certainly is true. However, if we argue, for example, that Christ's divine nature necessarily and always acts through the human nature, thus enabling him to perform miracles, a serious problem emerges concerning the plethora of texts that speak of the Holy Spirit's role in the life of Christ. This was the problem that Cyril's position was unable to fully overcome. By affirming that the Logos was the sole effective agent working on the human nature, Cyril's asymmetrical relation between the two natures rendered the Holy Spirit's work in the life of Jesus basically superfluous. Even Socinian theologians in the seventeenth century recognized this tension in classical Christology. What was the point of the Holy Spirit being given to Christ, they asked, if he is fully God?

The Christological genius of John Owen (1616–1683) becomes evident at precisely this point. Neither Roman Catholic nor Lutheran theologians can adequately account for any meaningful role of the Holy Spirit in the life of Christ. Indeed, their account of the relation between the two natures cannot sufficiently explain why Christ received the Holy Spirit without measure. Roman Catholic and Lutheran theologians generally do not know what to do with Christ's gifts and graces (e.g., faith and hope). However, Owen, as well as others, had his own way of explaining the relation of Christ's two natures. To my knowledge, this had not been as clearly articulated by anyone before him. One of his chief concerns was to protect the integrity of Christ's two natures. In so doing he made a rather bold contention that the only singular immediate act of the Son of God on the human nature was taking it into subsistence with himself. Every other act upon Christ's human nature was from the Holy Spirit. Christ performed his miracles through the power of the Holy Spirit, not immediately by his own divine power.

In other words, the divine nature acted not immediately by virtue of the hypostatic union, but mediately by means of the

Holy Spirit. The conventional way of understanding Christ's miracles has typically been to argue that Christ performs miracles by virtue of his own divine nature. But on Owen's (and others') model, the Holy Spirit is the immediate author of Christ's graces. This manner of understanding the relation of the Spirit to the human nature preserves the humanness of Jesus Christ and answers a host of exegetical questions.

It seems that some Christians imagine that Christ's divine nature takes the place of his soul. This idea, though well intended, is wrong. Christ was a perfect man with a rational soul as the immediate principle of his moral actions. In other words, Christ had a human self-consciousness. Some might say that the person of the Son is Christ's self-consciousness, but as some Reformed theologians argued, personality is not an act but the mode or identity of a thing. Importantly, Christ's humanity, both body and soul, does not get lost in his divinity. Because of this, Christ's humanity needed the Holy Spirit in order to have communion with God. His prayers to God were never simply the prayers of a man, nor even the prayers of the God-man to the Father; but more specifically they were the prayers of the Son of God to the Father in the power of the Spirit. Never was a prayer uttered before God from the lips of Christ that did not have the Holy Spirit working powerfully in his human nature to enable him to speak the words the Father had given him to speak. In this way, we aim to pray as our Lord prayed: in the Spirit.

Christ's inseparable companion during his earthly ministry as a true man was the Holy Spirit. Therefore, at all of the major events in the life of Christ, the Holy Spirit took a prominent role. The Holy Spirit was the immediate divine efficient cause of the incarnation (Matt. 1:18, 20; Luke 1:35). This was a fitting "beginning" for Christ since Isaiah spoke of the Messiah as one endowed with the Spirit (Isa. 42:1; 61:1).

The New Testament confirms Isaiah's testimony in several places, noting, for example, that Christ received the Spirit without measure (John 3:34). At Jesus's baptism the Spirit descended upon him (Matt. 3:16); and in Luke 4 the Spirit plays a significant role in leading Christ to and sustaining him before, during, and after his temptation (vv. 1, 14). In that same chapter Jesus reads from Isaiah 61:1–2 ("the Spirit of the Lord is upon me") and announces that he is the fulfillment of that prophecy (Luke 4:21). Christ performed miracles in the power of the Holy Spirit (Matt. 12:18; Acts 10:38). Hebrews 9:14 may be taken to mean that Christ offered himself up not by his own spirit but by the enabling of the Holy Spirit. Like his death, Christ's resurrection is attributed to the Holy Spirit (Rom. 8:11), and by it he "was declared to be the Son of God . . . according to the Spirit of holiness" (Rom. 1:4; see also 1 Tim. 3:16; 1 Pet. 3:18). Because the Spirit was Christ's inseparable companion during his earthly ministry, there is little doubt that Christ called out (i.e., prayed) to his Father by the enabling of the Spirit, which would put an implicit Christological emphasis upon Romans 8:26–27. The preponderance of references to the role of the Holy Spirit in the ministry of Christ finds its best explanation in the Reformed interpretative tradition.

Conclusion

Given the basic Christology above, Hugh Martin (1821–1885) argued that Jesus

> inevitably placed himself, therefore, in a position of ac-
> knowledged weakness and infirmity—of absolute depen-
> dence on God—a dependence to be exercised and expressed

in the adorations and supplications of prayer. He was made of a woman, made under the law—under the law of prayer, as of other ordinances and duties—the law by which a man can receive nothing except it be given him from heaven, and except the Lord be inquired of for it (Ezek. 36:37).[3]

Christ exercised, according to his human nature, faith, love, reverence, delight, and all the graces proper to a true human nature in the power of the Holy Spirit. Thus, he naturally would have desired to offer vocal requests and supplications to his Father in heaven. He would have also praised God with the knowledge he had of his Father. Additionally, he would have sought God out with a holy determination, making all other duties subservient to the duty of communion with God. In other words, true and proper humanity is realized only in communion with God.

For Christ to forsake prayer would have detracted from his true humanity. But, as we shall see, his devotion to God in prayer argues otherwise. That God truly became flesh (John 1:14) is powerfully manifested in our praying Lord.

1

Jesus Prayed from His Mother's Breasts

Psalm 22:9–10

Yet you are he who took me from the womb;
    you made me trust you at my mother's breasts.
On you was I cast from my birth,
    and from my mother's womb you have been my God.

A Holy Beginning

Given what we know about Christ's parents, particularly his mother Mary, the "favored one" (Luke 1:28), there can be little doubt that our Lord was raised in a pious, God-fearing household. All of the advantages that he needed to be a faithful Mediator were graciously bestowed upon him from his heavenly Father. Naturally, that would have included a family that raised him to know and love the Lord his God. Jesus was a faithful covenant child, a true Israelite in whom there was no deceit.

A child raised in a God-fearing household receives an inestimable blessing. True, to whom much is given much will be required (Luke 12:48). And in the case of the Lord Jesus, much was required of him, which means much was given to him. As we read in Psalm 84:11:

> For the LORD God is a sun and shield;
>> the LORD bestows favor and honor.
> No good thing does he withhold
>> from those who walk uprightly.

God delighted in blessing his only begotten Son from conception and will do so for all eternity.

In the first place, Jesus was a child of the covenant. He was not raised in a pagan environment, having to fend for himself in terms of his religious life.[1] Rather, circumcised on the eighth day, he not only possessed the sign of the covenant—a sign of God's covenant faithfulness to his people (Rom. 4:11)—but also received a name that was to be a badge, daily reminding him of his extraordinarily high calling as God's Messiah (Luke 2:21). This was to affirm Christ's solidarity with his father (Joseph) and the covenantal community of which he was a part. Not even our Lord entered the world as a neutral individual. Rather, he was in corporate solidarity with the community of faith (Gal. 3:16–29).

Just as our own identity leads to action, so too with Christ: his identity was the ground for how he lived. "Be who you are" is a statement true of Christ himself and thereby fitting also for his holy people (i.e., we are holy, so we live holy lives).

The key to understanding Christ's religious life from the womb is to insist that his faith was not solely for him but also for others (i.e., his people). Remember, Christ is the natural Son of God, so his adoption is never in question: he belongs to God. He would impart his own spiritual blessings (e.g., faith, hope, love) to his people by sending his Spirit into their hearts (see John 14–16).

His religious life began from the womb. Psalm 22 finds its ultimate fulfillment in Christ, though its immediate story is that of David. The Father prepared a body for Christ, which was formed by the Spirit in the womb of the Virgin Mary. According to the natural limits of his humanity, Christ's early prayer life was clearly not as developed as it would be at the end of his life. Experience is a great teacher for our prayers, and the more he experienced, the more his prayers would develop in light of those experiences, challenges, and struggles.

Whatever acts of consent were possible toward the Father, involving the deliberate use of his human will, Christ performed perfectly, but also appropriately according to his age and stage in life. His acts of reason were married together with the holy principles in his heart formed by the Holy Spirit. His heart, soul, mind, and strength all directed his actions in a manner appropriate to his age and capacity for spiritual acts of reason. He possessed the habit of faith from the womb, which would then bring forth particular acts of faith at the appropriate time in response to God and his Word.

God took Christ "from the womb" and "made" him trust at his mother's breasts (Ps. 22:9). Christ trusted God, but not as though he alone was responsible for his acts of faith toward God. Rather, the Father sustained him so that Christ's religious life was faithful from the womb to the tomb. In another psalm the reality of spiritual life from the very beginning of our existence comes into focus:

> For you, O Lord, are my hope,
>   my trust, O LORD, from my youth.

Upon you I have leaned from before my birth;
>   you are he who took me from my mother's womb.
My praise is continually of you. (Ps. 71:5–6)

If these words are true of the psalmist, how much more are they true of the Son of God! Christ not only trusted from his youth but also leaned on God from before birth. How very different is this Hebrew idea of spirituality, which allows for and celebrates the faith of children from the womb, compared with our rationalistic views today.

We may appreciate the reality of the spiritual life of the young because God is the initiator of true spirituality, and we are not. The Father is never shy regarding his help toward his Son, the righteous servant.

Behold my servant, whom I uphold,
>   my chosen, in whom my soul delights;
I have put my Spirit upon him;
>   he will bring forth justice to the nations. (Isa. 42:1)

God upheld his Son in order that the Son, whether eating or drinking, might bring glory to God (1 Cor. 10:31). As the Son was cast upon the Father from birth, there was never a time when the Father was not his God (Ps. 22:10). Not only Psalm 22 but also Psalm 8 speaks of the reality of Christ's religious life from the womb:

>   Out of the mouth of babies and infants,
you have established strength because of your foes,
>   to still the enemy and the avenger. (Ps. 8:2)

Charles Spurgeon (1834–1892) asks, "Was our Lord so early a believer? Was he one of those babes and sucklings out of whose mouths strength is ordained? So it would seem; and

30

if so, what a plea for help!"[2] Our Lord, the pioneer of our faith (Heb. 12:2)—meaning he himself lived by faith in God—was never without the graces of faith, hope, and love. As John Calvin (1509–1564) argued:

> Truly, Christ was sanctified from earliest infancy in order that he might sanctify in himself his elect from every age without distinction. . . . Thus, he was conceived of the Holy Spirit in order that, in the flesh taken, fully imbued with the holiness of the Spirit, he might impart that holiness to us. If we have in Christ the most perfect example of all the graces which God bestows upon his children, in this respect also he will be for us a proof that the age of infancy is not utterly averse to sanctification.[3]

In other words, the holy life of Christ from the beginning, we are told, was one of conscious awareness of God because God made it so. Jesus's life of dependence on and awareness of God his Father was axiomatic to his existence as a true human being made in God's image and sustained by the Spirit of the living God. As natural as it was for him to breath God's air, so too he found it the most natural thing in the world to look to God, by faith, in order to know him and delight in him. Truly, if anyone prayed without ceasing—from his first breath to his last—it was Jesus of Nazareth (1 Thess. 5:17).

A Holy Teenager

As Jesus grew older, we are told, he became "strong, filled with wisdom"—God's favor (grace) was upon him (Luke 2:40). By age twelve Jesus would have possessed a deep knowledge of God, but a knowledge filled with filial devotion to his heavenly Father. The temple incident in Luke 2, when Jesus remained in Jerusalem, shows that he was asking and answering questions that amazed others (vv. 46–47). After a rebuke from his parents, who had been searching for him for days, Jesus informed them that he was doing what was appropriate: "Did you not know that I must be in my Father's house?" (v. 49). After this, Luke informs his readers that Jesus "increased in wisdom and in stature and in favor with God and man" (v. 52).

God comes first. This was the radical principle of Christ's actions during his life. Not his parents' will, however important it was for him to be submissive to them; not his own will, however natural a thing that would be for a holy, undefiled person; but the will of his Father was omnipotent in the life of the Son of God.

Speaking of Christ's earlier years, David M. M'Intyre suggests that Christ would

> join not only in the worship of the home, but also in the prayers of the synagogue, breathing into them, without doubt, a deeper meaning than that which lay in the mere letter of the word, as He supplicated Heaven's mercy, not only on His fellow-townsmen of Nazareth, but on all the people of Israel and on the Seventy Nations beyond.[4]

What a story the youth of our Savior would be, with his faithful allegiance to Yahweh each day as preparation for his public ministry.

The habits of grace overflowed in his heart, giving him the perpetual knowledge that he must be about his Father's business. So in whatever context he found himself, the prayers of young Jesus would have been a great delight to him as his Father prepared him, morning by morning (Isa. 50:4–6), for the battle that would quickly come to the One who alone could bring many sons to glory (Heb. 2:10).

Given that Christ's public ministry did not formally begin until he was baptized, we may, without too much speculation, conjecture that his private life was one of regular, fervent prayer in the presence of his Father. God so endowed his Son with the Spirit of holiness that the preparation of the Messiah in large part took place in the school of communion with God.

A Holy Pattern

Just as there seems to be no reason to doubt the spontaneous, free, and natural pattern of Christ's occasional prayers as he grew up, there seems no good reason to doubt that the shape for Christ's own prayer life came from the Psalms. Consider, for example, the language of Psalm 17 and how the words were especially designed for him to pray to his Father. After all, if David could say these words with integrity, how much more the One who was without sin!

> Hear a just cause, O LORD; attend to my cry!
>> Give ear to my prayer from lips free of deceit!
> From your presence let my vindication come!
>> Let your eyes behold the right!
>
> You have tried my heart, you have visited me by night,
>> you have tested me, and you will find nothing;
>> I have purposed that my mouth will not transgress. . . .
>
> Keep me as the apple of your eye;
>> hide me in the shadow of your wings. . . .
>
> As for me, I shall behold your face in righteousness;
>> when I awake, I shall be satisfied with your likeness.
>>> (vv. 1–3, 8, 15)

No one could pray these words in quite the same way as our Savior. He alone was truly free of deceit. So his desire for vindication (1 Tim. 3:16) was natural. Christ purposed that his mouth would not transgress (Ps. 17:3)—a prayer that highlights the backbone of our salvation. The One with whom the Father publicly declared he was well pleased was the same One who had prayed that God would keep him as the apple of his eye (Ps. 17:8). With such an intimate relationship, Christ beheld the face of God and was satisfied with his likeness (Ps. 17:15).

We may go even further: the words of the Psalms are the words of the Son of God. What the Son had declared to his people through the Spirit in the Psalms of the Old Testament he now takes to his (human) lips as he makes use of the words that he himself brought about through the experiences, trials, joys, and sufferings of his servants. What an amazing thought that Christ should prepare words for himself to use in his own prayers.

Our Lord came into this world with the graces needed to live out his calling as the Son of God. As such, he had not only the abilities to live in constant communion with God, but also the identity that he was someone peculiar: the God-man. Such abilities and awareness, coupled with the Father's resolve to have his Son know him, provide us with the proper context for the prayers of Jesus and why his life was lived in constant communion with his heavenly Father. Furnished with the Spirit, his life was a constant Trinitarian activity: the Son communing with the Father in the power of the Spirit. Just as he first called upon the Lord by the power of the Spirit working upon his human nature, so his last words were calling upon the Lord by the Spirit (Luke 23:46; Heb. 9:14).

We should note the importance of starting well in life: it is easier to develop patterns and habits at an early age than to pick up those habits later in life for the first time. For some this is not possible, due to their life circumstances (e.g., growing up in a non-Christian household). But in believing households, children must therefore be taught to pray, by faith, as early as possible and as frequently as they are able. In Scripture there are patterns for us to follow, words for us to use to help us in our prayers. God does not expect his own Son to be left alone to figure out how to pray. Thus, he certainly would not leave us to ourselves in so important a spiritual discipline.

2

Jesus Prayed "Abba! Father"

John 17:1

Father, the hour has come; glorify your
Son that the Son may glorify you.

My Father

The first recorded words of Jesus in Luke 2 speak of his allegiance to his Father when he tells of his business in his Father's house. The last recorded words of Jesus speak of his trust in his Father as he cries out, "'Father, into your hands I commit my spirit!'" And, Luke adds, "having said this he breathed his last" (Luke 23:46).

Any study on the prayer life of the Son of God must take into account the fact, especially observed in the Gospel accounts, that Jesus habitually and fervently prayed to his Father in heaven. This may at first seem to us to be quite ordinary, until we probe further.

Referring to God in prayer as "my Father" was virtually unheard of during Christ's time. Jews typically referred to God in prayer as "Yahweh," "my Lord," "my God," or "God of my father." The words of Christ simply have no precedence: "At that time Jesus declared, 'I thank you, Father, Lord of heaven and earth . . .'" (Matt. 11:25). As New Testament scholar Joachim Jeremias says, "We can say quite deliberately that there is no analogy at all in the whole literature of Jewish prayer for God being addressed as Abba. This assertion applies not only to fixed liturgical prayer, but also to free prayer, of which many examples have been handed down to us in Talmudic literature."[1]

Thus, Jesus revolutionized prayer in a way that did justice to the radical nature of his ministry. With no previous examples of faithful Jews addressing God as "Father" in prayer, the supremely faithful Jew referred to God as "Father" almost exclusively in his recorded prayers. There must have been a very good reason for this development.

The Aramaic word *abba* refers to a father-child relationship. Before Christ's time, Aramaic-speaking children would learn to refer to their parents as *abba* and *imma*. During Christ's life, not only small children but also grown children would refer to their fathers as *abba*. Yet, to address God as *abba* would have been deemed disrespectful by Jews. What our Lord did was new and, as I said, revolutionary in how to approach God. If Jesus were not who he was, we would have grounds for joining with the Jews in accusing him of blasphemy: "This was why the Jews were seeking all the more to kill him, because not only was he breaking the Sabbath, but he was even calling God his own Father, making himself equal with God" (John 5:18).

Because of Jesus's unique and therefore special relationship to the Father, it remains most appropriate to address him as such. As the eternal Son of the Father, he enjoyed an intimate relationship with the Father that manifests itself clearly in the audible prayer of Matthew 11:27: "All things have been handed over to me by my Father, and no one knows the Son except the Father, and no one knows the Father except the Son and anyone to whom the Son chooses to reveal him." Given the intimacy clearly revealed in the mutual knowledge that the Father and Son possessed of one another, Jesus rightly related to him as Father and paved the way for us to do the same.

Consider, as well, that because of the uniqueness of the eternal relationship between persons of the Trinity, Christ addressed God as Father in practically all circumstances, even the most dire: "My Father, if it be possible, let this cup pass from me; nevertheless, not as I will, but as you will" (Matt. 26:39). This bold request from the incarnate Christ found its impetus in the infinite intimacy with which he related to the Father from eternity. At the same time, the arrival of the Son in the flesh provided a new way of relating to God. Prayer became a deeply intimate conversation between God the Father and his people because of Christ's person and work in bringing us to such a place.

The Spirit of Adoption

Besides his unique relationship to the Father as the Son of God, Jesus also called upon the Father through the powerful indwelling presence of the Holy Spirit. We find the Spirit referred to as the Spirit not only of the Father (Matt. 10:20) but also of the Son (Gal. 4:6). The Spirit provides the bond of the Trinity and, with it, the union of love between the Father and the Son.

Thus, it should come as little surprise to us that in his earthly ministry as the God-man, the Messiah manifested himself as the man of the Spirit *par excellence*. Indeed, Isaiah foretold this hundreds of years before the birth of Christ:

> And the Spirit of the LORD shall rest upon him,
>   the Spirit of wisdom and understanding,
>   the Spirit of counsel and might,
>   the Spirit of knowledge and the fear of the LORD.
>   (Isa. 11:2)

> Behold my servant, whom I uphold,
>   my chosen, in whom my soul delights;
> I have put my Spirit upon him;
>   he will bring forth justice to the nations. (Isa. 42:1)

> The Spirit of the Lord GOD is upon me,
>   because the LORD has anointed me
> to bring good news to the poor. (Isa. 61:1)

The Holy Spirit related to Christ as his inseparable earthly and (even now more so) heavenly companion. He was poured into Christ's heart that Christ might naturally, frequently, and joyfully call upon God as "Abba! Father!" (Rom. 8:15). The Spirit bore witness to his spirit that he was the Son of God (cf. Rom. 8:16). The Spirit bears witness to us that we are children of God; but this is true only because the Spirit comes from the hand of Christ who enables us to share in the joy he had as the Son of God.

Given the intimacy of his relationship to the Father, Christ would have experienced the deepest agony, frustration, and unhappiness if he could not call upon him as such. It would have constituted an essential denial of "paternity." But since no one else can claim existence as the Only Begotten of the Father,

Christ possessed the unique joy and privilege of revealing God in this manner to those aware of his messianic calling.

Charles Spurgeon says, "If any man of woman born might have lived without prayer it was surely the Lord Jesus Christ."[2] Rather, should we not maintain the exact opposite? While it is true that we, who have remaining sin, need to pray, there was a necessity placed upon Christ to pray because of his natural relation to the Father. Likewise, the powerful indwelling of the Spirit provoked within him a habitual cry for communion.

Adam as the son of God had happiness, since he knew that he received perfect gifts as a son from a father. The relationship was not merely one of love but also one of a Father's love for his son. The Father gave Adam the Holy Spirit for this purpose, just as he did the last Adam, Jesus Christ, for whom he confirmed his blessed fatherly relationship. We, through Christ, enter into this "confirmation" from the work of the Spirit, who definitely and perpetually seals our relationship to God (Eph. 1:13–14).

Union with the Son

Jesus taught his disciples to pray, "Our Father in heaven . . ." (Matt. 6:9). The Son of God to whom we are united by faith makes this special title for addressing God possible. Christ's eternal and natural sonship provides the foundation for the adoption of believers, who call upon God as Father as part of his family (Eph. 1:5; 2:19). As adopted children of God, we belong to his, not Satan's, family. Our attitude toward God in prayer arises out of our standing before him as his children.

Strikingly, our Lord joins our sonship to his own in John 20:17, when he says to Mary, "Do not cling to me, for I have not yet ascended to the Father; but go to my brothers and say to them, 'I am ascending to my Father and your Father, to my God and your God.'"

Our salvation has many benefits, one of which includes God sending the "Spirit of his Son into our hearts, crying, 'Abba! Father!'" (Gal. 4:6). Just as Christ cried, "Abba! Father" (Mark 14:36) by the power of the Spirit, we must and will do the same.

This privilege of address by faith, in union with Christ, by the power of the Spirit, will never end. Even in the world to come, our "familiar conversation with God," as many loosely call prayer, will remain forever. Our residence in heaven with our Father and Savior will in no way change our relation to him as children of God. With that in mind, Christ, as the heavenly God-man, keeps perpetually the joy of calling upon and maintaining communion with his Father, even as he so beautifully displayed by faith on earth.

3

Jesus Prayed in Secret

Luke 5:16

But he would withdraw to desolate places and pray.

Intentional Private Devotion

With such an abundance of love for his Father, Jesus sought him in secret for the reward of joyous fellowship arising out of such an intimate approach. After all, our Lord says, "But when you pray, go into your room and shut the door and pray to your Father who is in secret. And your Father who sees in secret will reward you" (Matt. 6:6). Jesus took this reality seriously, as the Father rewards those who, believing he exists, seek him (Heb. 11:6).

Numerous Synoptic Gospel references highlight Christ's prayers: Matthew 14:23; Mark 1:35; 6:46; 14:36; Luke 3:21; 5:16; 6:12; 9:18, 28ff. Jesus represents a new "Daniel," the first Daniel having pointed to Christ when he "went to his house" and "got down on his knees three times a day and prayed and gave thanks before his God, as he had done previously" (Dan. 6:10). Daniel prayed in a crisis here, but in connection with a common pattern of personal piety before the Lord. As we would expect, our Savior manifested the grace of this Old Testament prophet in a much superior abundance. Indeed, he necessarily exhibited far greater communion, quantitatively and qualitatively, than any saint we encounter in the Bible.

Early in the Morning

Jews began their day with prayer, the first order of business of dependent, faithful, believers in the true and living God. Many Christians today are more likely to check their phones as the first priority. Instead of communing with God, we naturally prefer to "commune" with other humans, some of whom we do not even know (e.g., on Facebook).

As a faithful Jew, Jesus rose "very early in the morning, while it was still dark," and went to pray in a "desolate place" (Mark 1:35). He left Capernaum to pray alone. Here, Mark possibly likens this act to Israel's sojourn in the wilderness, where they should have fellowshiped with God. Interestingly, Jesus's prayers in Mark's Gospel are always solitary (1:35; 6:46; 14:32–39) and in connection to either explicit or implicit opposition to his ministry. Action, in the form of compassion, immediately followed his prayers and suggests that Jesus never took matters purely into his own hands. He always performed the will of the Father while seeking him in a spirit of total dependence, evidenced by his prayers. He sought guidance and confirmation that he was indeed doing his Father's will, which explains in part his rigorous and sustained prayer life.

New Testament accounts clearly show that Jesus lived neither as a reclusive hermit nor as a maniacal social butterfly. He manifested himself as both a highly visible public and a behind-the-scenes private man. As is often the case, public faithfulness or failure remains directly proportional to the faithfulness or failure in private. Jesus knew that these tendencies went together. Few run a publicly good race to the end in their ministries who have not been faithful in private with their covenant God.

Often in the moral failures of evangelical leaders, public failure arises not out of a vacuum but from behind closed doors. A public fiasco always involves a private mess. Not so with our Savior. His public ministry before God depended intimately on his private communion with him. One without the other would have proved fatal.

In many contexts, Christ withdrew to pray not only for communion with the Father but also in the sense that his disciples lacked understanding regarding his mission. He would need to pray not only for his own understanding of God's will but also for their understanding of God's will because of the crucial role they would eventually end up playing in God's purposes. "Your will be done" was never an exclusive request for himself but was also for others to join with him in accomplishing the will of God.

Times of crisis usually bring us to prayer more than anything else in the world. They come as gifts from God to prompt our acceptance of personal weakness and limitations in order that we may depend on his immeasurable power and provision. That was, in a sense, true of Christ, who faced many calamities connected to not only his enemies but also his friends. In the end, he knew that all of these trials came ultimately from his sovereign Lord. Jesus was "weak" in the sense that he had to faithfully tread the path set by his Father, which led to his being crucified in weakness (2 Cor. 13:4). In other words, we ourselves are "weak" when we give up control and hand it over to God; but, of course, like Christ, that is when we are truly strong! Praise God for crises, both large and small: they bring us to him and reveal our weakness.

Christ Alone

Luke also records several instances of Christ praying, often alone:

- "Now when all the people were baptized, and when Jesus also had been baptized and was praying, the heavens were opened" (Luke 3:21).
- "And when it was day, he departed and went into a desolate place . . ." (Luke 4:42).
- "But he would withdraw to desolate places and pray" (Luke 5:16).
- "In these days he went out to the mountain to pray, and all night he continued in prayer to God" (Luke 6:12).
- "Now it happened that as he was praying alone, the disciples were with him. And he asked them, 'Who do the crowds say that I am?'" (Luke 9:18).
- "Now about eight days after these sayings he took with him Peter and John and James and went up on the mountain to pray" (Luke 9:28).

Matthew does the same:

- "And after he had dismissed the crowds, he went up on the mountain by himself to pray. When evening came, he was there alone" (Matt. 14:23).
- "Then Jesus went with them to a place called Gethsemane, and he said to his disciples, 'Sit here, while I go over there and pray'" (Matt. 26:36).

Not all of the references to Christ's prayers denote solitary ones. Nonetheless, the Gospel writers frequently make mention of Christ purposefully withdrawing to spend time with his heavenly Father. Surely, these records exist not simply for our observation but also for our observance. The godly life, we may say, involves both public worship and private communion, as Christ exhibited on our behalf and for our example.

Prayer as Preparation

One particularly striking reference in Luke speaks of Jesus praying all night: "In these days he went out to the mountain to pray, and all night he continued in prayer to God" (Luke 6:12). When one considers how many Christians today struggle to maintain more than a few minutes in sustained prayer with God at one time, this account rattles most of us. We need not remain in such a condition. Let us begin by marveling how Christ always placed the needs of the kingdom and us before his own, even if it meant sleepless nights. Let us then prayerfully determine to do the same out of devotion to him and others.

The mountain was a place not only for isolation but also where theophanies and divine revelations took place as revealed in Jewish literature (e.g., Exodus 19). Certainly, Christ's choice of the Twelve established a new leadership in Israel while censuring the (blind) religious leaders of the day—a choice made not alone but in line with his Father's will. In spite of the close communion Jesus would develop with these twelve men, he also knew that one would betray him unto death. These significant choices for Jesus on behalf of his people demanded intense prayer as he simultaneously embraced the Father's will and prepared for the treachery to come at the hands of Judas.

Later on, Jesus asked his disciples, whom he had chosen through prayer, concerning "who" he was (Luke 9:18, 20). Was he praying that they would recognize his messianic identity? If so, he got his answer with Peter's confession of him as "the Christ of God" (v. 20). Far from such an answer prompting Jesus to pride, it would remind him of the misery to come for God's Messiah. Thus, immediately after Peter's confession, Christ reminded them, "The Son of Man must suffer many things and be rejected by the elders and chief priests and scribes, and be killed, and on the third day be raised" (v. 22). Contrary to the desires of the people for a conquering Messiah, Jesus knew that the path to triumph necessarily led through the valley of humiliation. Prayer prepared him for this.

Rewarded

In Matthew 6:6 Jesus promises his disciples that their Father will reward them when they pray in secret. In that one chapter, the word *reward* occurs seven times, which unquestionably points us to the blessings our Father gives in response to private prayer.

We do not have because we do not ask (James 4:2), and that exposes our lack of faith (Matt. 21:22). Christ asked because he had such strong faith. In turn, he wants to draw us near to God in faith, believing that he exists and that he will reward those who seek him (Heb. 11:6). As we see in John's Gospel, Jesus believed God existed, drew near to him, and also prayed for his reward: "And now, Father, glorify me in your own presence with the glory that I had with you before the world existed" (John 17:5). We must do likewise, as long as we do so biblically.

We struggle when it comes to private prayer. Jonathan Edwards (1703–1758) wrote a sermon "Hypocrites Deficient in the Duty of Prayer," which in some respects stirs up more conviction than his justly famous sermon "Sinners in the Hands of an Angry God." Ordinarily, false converts are the ones deficient in private prayer. Yet, even the most godly saints find quality prayer in private a toil. With this in mind, let us look for help to the godliest man ever, our Lord Jesus Christ, a man of private prayer.

Some emphasize the idea of a Christian's "quiet time" at the expense of the more important duty of public worship. Others so prioritize corporate worship that they minimize the role of private prayer. Instead, we must see this not as an either–or but as a both–and matter. Our triune God, who meets with us in a glorious way at corporate worship, also remains pleased to commune with us anytime during the course of our daily lives, especially in private prayer. Jesus spent time not only in the synagogue and temple but also in private communion. The former should naturally lead to the latter. Private and public worship are friends that help each other.

4

Jesus Prayed the Lord's Prayer

Matthew 6:9–13

Our Father in heaven,
hallowed be your name.
Your kingdom come,
your will be done,
    on earth as it is in heaven.
Give us this day our daily bread,
and forgive us our debts,
    as we also have forgiven our debtors.
And lead us not into temptation,
    but deliver us from evil.

The Lord's Prayer

In the Gospels, the disciples never request instruction on preaching from their Master, but they do ask him to teach them how to pray. We must not think that the disciples knew nothing about prayer. In actual fact, set forms of prayer often identified formal religious groups in biblical times, such as John the Baptist and his disciples (Luke 11:1). So, by asking Jesus "how to pray," they were possibly asking for a specific form of prayer to distinguish them from others. Jesus offers a prayer that incorporates a whole body of divinity and provides fundamental teachings he gives as the prophesied Prophet (Deut. 18:18).

It is hard to overstate the significance of the Lord's Prayer in the life of the church. Up until the fifth century many Christian churches incorporated it into their liturgy, often right before the Lord's Supper. In the *Didache* ("The Teaching of the Twelve Apostles"), a late first-century document, we find the Lord's Prayer cited word for word. The *Didache* exhorts Christians to pray it three times daily. The prayer was meant for full members of the church, not pagans. This breathtaking prayer must flow from the lips of the godly, not only in the actual words but also with its larger intended meaning, which therefore allows for other words not explicitly found in it.[1]

We may ask a rather simple but profound question about the Lord's Prayer. Did Jesus actually pray it in the context when he taught it? Many of us assume, without perhaps thinking through the matter carefully enough, that his words were purely didactic (for teaching purposes only). But it seems unlikely that Christ would have so divided teaching and doxology here. He probably taught it not only with words of instruction but also with a prayer by example. In other words, he offered the prayer to his heavenly Father while simultaneously teaching it.

Heavenly Father

Before we get to the petitions, we must not miss the address, "Our Father in heaven," which Christians in prayer can quickly pass over without a thought. "Heavenly" draws our minds to

God's transcendence; "Father" assures us of his immanence. In history, Christianity alone maintains the balance. God is separate but not distant, incomprehensible but attainable. This sets before us the supreme example of a reverent approach to prayer. He is not our buddy, the big sugar daddy in the sky. Neither is he a capricious and fatalistic despot we may not approach with intimacy and confidence. He is our heavenly Father, above us and beyond us in all ways, yet amazingly close at hand. Jesus approached his Father with reverence and intimacy at the same time. So must we. Indeed, our reverence toward God stems from the fact that he is attainable and near to us.

The First Petition: "Hallowed Be Your Name"

The first petition expresses Christ's longing for God's name to be magnified and held in honor as he brings glory to it. The petition essentially craves that the Father's name be sanctified, set apart as holy, which it truly is. The one who wants God's name to be hallowed wants holiness for himself. Jesus pursued both of these in thought, word, and deed throughout his entire life on earth. In John 7:18, for example, he affirms that he speaks not on his own authority but on his Father's. In this way, he seeks not his own but his Father's glory. Thus, in his High Priestly Prayer to his Father at the end of his life (John 17), Christ drew attention to the honor he so bountifully rendered: "I glorified you on earth, having accomplished the work that you gave me to do" (v. 4).

We must not miss how crucial it was that our Lord perfectly brought honor to God's name as he paved the way for us to do the same through him. Apart from Christ uttering these words before the Father, and living a life consistent with this petition, we would have no hope of bringing glory to God, which is the first and most important commandment. When we truly desire that God's name be honored, we are expressing the longing that our lives be holy. In a sense, when we pray, "Hallowed be your name," we are praying, "Set us apart unto you, that your name be set apart as holy."

The words of Psalm 8:1 are ultimately from Christ for Christ to use so that he would have the privilege of hallowing his Father's name:

> O LORD, our Lord,
>> how majestic is your name in all the earth!
> You have set your glory above the heavens.

Second Petition: "Your Kingdom Come"

Jesus came to destroy "the works of the devil" (1 John 3:8). There were a number of previews (e.g., his temptation) to the finale whereby Christ would conquer Satan at Calvary. But at the cross, the Son of God crushed the head of the Serpent (Gen. 3:15), who held the power of death (Heb. 2:14). "Christ the Victor" rose again in triumph to swallow up death! This provided the way for Jews and Gentiles to be brought into God's kingdom and enter into this victory with him. It was a truly cosmic conquest, infinitely beyond even the greatest human triumph there ever was or shall be.

When Christ prayed for the advancement of God's kingdom, he had already been advancing it, and in a way the disciples barely understood (Mark 1:15). He alone understood what was required for the progress of God's kingdom on earth: his death. Conquest as a King came not by subduing but by suffering. His life was a perpetual Gethsemane as he continually faced the reality of his unjustly violent, utterly shameful, and bitterly lonesome death.

This petition of Christ's has an obvious ongoing efficacy as he discharges to the church, through his apostles, prophets, ministers, elders, deacons, and others, the work that increases God's reign on earth.

> When [Jesus] ascended on high he led a host of captives,
> and he gave gifts to men. (Eph. 4:8)

As John Stott says, "Christ ascended as conqueror to the Father's right hand, his train of captives being the principalities and powers he had defeated, dethroned and disarmed."[2]

His victory was sure, but the intent of his prayer involved continuing kingdom work to be accomplished by the church in utter dependence on the One who alone could accomplish it. Without this petition, not only is there no salvation, but also there is no point to the church. With these words coming from the lips of Christ himself we have confidence that our labor is not in vain (1 Cor. 15:58), for the victory is ours in Christ.

Third Petition: "Your Will Be Done . . ."

Following "Your kingdom come," the next petition comprised the very fiber of Christ's spiritual DNA. The Son left heaven, not with the purpose of doing his own will, but in order to do the will of the Father (John 6:38). He gave up his prerogatives and relied entirely upon the Holy Spirit to direct him in his obedience to God. Hence, Christ says: "I can do nothing on my own. As I hear, I judge, and my judgment is just, because I seek not my own will but the will of him who sent me" (John 5:30; see also 4:34).

Our Lord, by virtue of the covenant he made with the Father concerning the salvation of the elect, fulfilled the will of God generally by keeping the law (both the Old Testament ceremonial and moral aspects of it). At the same time, he completed the law by observing "positive" laws, pertaining to his office as Prophet, Priest, and King. Of course, in Gethsemane we note Christ wrestling with the Father's specific will related to drinking the bitter and agonizing cup of God's wrath. He asked three times for the cup to be removed but each time acknowledged freely that God's will, not his own, must be done (Matt. 26:42, 44).

The angels in heaven know what it is to do the will of God perfectly. Still, even they do not fully comprehend the meaning and magnitude of the Son's observance of it and the conditions he endured to do so. They can only worship in amazement at what God's Son suffered in order to remain in the Father's love (John 15:10). Not only did Jesus do the Father's will in all things, under sometimes horrendous circumstances, but he also accomplished it joyfully, constantly, zealously, and completely—from the heart, by faith, to the glory of God.

If there was ever a perfect example of the will of God being done on earth as it is in heaven, Jesus was that example.

Fourth Petition: "Give Us This Day Our Daily Bread"

Jesus gave thanks in all circumstances, just as Paul would later exhort believers (1 Thess. 5:18). What makes this even more remarkable is the fact that Jesus upholds all things, owns all things, and knew that all things were not only made by him but also for him (Col. 1:16). Doing the will of the Father at all times gave cause for his thankfulness, because he knew that whatever he received came from the hand of his Father, whom he could trust.

The corporate nature of the Lord's Prayer is well known, even by the plain reading of the words. In John 6, Jesus feeds the five thousand through a miracle that he performed. Nonetheless, even though he miraculously fed thousands, our Lord gave thanks before he and the others ate (vv. 11, 23; see also Matt. 15:36; Luke 9:16). Did anyone eat a loaf of bread or a fish with as much true thankfulness as Christ?

But perhaps more significantly for our Lord, though one cannot rule out the sacramental context of John 6, he later in his ministry gave thanks at what has been called "the Lord's Supper." Luke informs us, "And he took a cup, and when he had given thanks he said, 'Take this, and divide it among yourselves'" (Luke 22:17). Then, after having tasted the fruit of the vine (i.e., wine), Jesus "took bread, and when he had given thanks, he broke it and gave it to them, saying, 'This is my body, which is given for you. Do this in remembrance of me'" (Luke 22:19). The disciples at the time did not fully grasp what was unfolding before their very eyes. Jesus did. He knew profoundly that the very bread and wine for which he gave thanks symbolized his body and blood very shortly to be sacrificed.

In an age where Christians are embarrassed at times to thank God for their supper in a public setting, the Son of God gave thanks for his death. Think about that. Prayers at restaurants do not need to be reenactments of Daniel 9, but a simple acknowledgment of thanksgiving to a good God is surely not out of the question, is it?

Fifth Petition: "Forgive Us Our Debts"

We might be justified in claiming that Jesus could not have prayed this petition, because he, the sinless Lamb of God, had no sins that needed forgiveness. I have some sympathy for such a response, but let us consider a few factors before dismissing the notion.

Jesus came into this world as a representative person. Like Adam's actions, the actions of Christ were representative (Rom. 5:12–21). At the beginning of his public ministry he submitted to John's baptism of repentance. In addition to thereby being publicly ordained to the ministry as Prophet, Priest, and King, he also identified with sinners, which would culminate at his baptism (Luke 12:50) "accomplished" on the cross. By receiving baptism from John, Jesus willingly took on the servant's role in solidarity with sinners, even though he never sinned.

In the same way, the blameless prophet Daniel manifested such corporate solidarity when he prayed corporately about Judah's sins that led to exile in Babylon. Yes, Daniel was a sinner, yet he was blameless of the infidelity that caused God to turn against his people. Still, he could pray, "We have sinned and done wrong and acted wickedly and rebelled, turning aside from your commandments and rules" (Dan. 9:5). Similarly (while not exactly!), Jesus could pray, "Forgive us our debts," in a way that asked God to forgive the debts of his people. Again, the corporate nature of this prayer is crucial to understanding why Jesus needed to pray these words. He was acting as Intercessor; he desired forgiveness for those with whom he identified, knowing that forgiveness would come only if he remained supremely faithful to the end.

Jesus would have prayed the Psalms of the Old Testament. In psalms that express confession of sin, he could not confess his sin individually, but he could make confession corporately. He could lament the sins of the world and join in by sympathizing with us in our weaknesses (Heb. 4:15).

Sixth Petition: "And Lead Us Not into Temptation"

In the sixth petition, again, we have a crucial component in the prayer life of Jesus, not only for his own needs but also for those of his people. This petition asks that God keep his people from being tempted to sin. And, moreover, if they are tempted, that they may, by the power of the Spirit, be supported and kept in the hour of temptation.

No human ever endured temptation even remotely to the same extent as our Lord Jesus Christ. He was tempted in every way (Heb. 4:15). Christ waged war against the Devil and vice versa. The Evil One knew that if our Lord fell even once, he would lose not just a battle but the entire war. Satan would have won the most hideously maleficent victory ever attained. Everything was at stake. Thus, Christ had to pray first that he would not fall into temptation, and then only could he ask that his people would be kept from the same. As noted, Jesus often prayed in private. It seems a case can be made that he often prayed in private when a sort of temptation to "fame" and immediate success appeared on the horizon. He needed to pray that he would not be tempted to get his glory the easy way from people who did not fully understand what it meant for Jesus to be King.

In another instance, Jesus commanded his disciples to "watch and pray," so that they would not enter into temptation (Matt. 26:41). He said this immediately before going to the Father for a second time while wrestling with the Father's will (to go to the cross) versus his own will (to have the "cup" removed from him) (Matt. 26:42–44). There was surely a temptation—in many respects, perfectly natural and obvious—for Christ wanting to avoid Golgotha. But his temptation was not in accordance with the will of God, and so he prayed and found that God's will was for him to die in the place of sinners.

Jesus prepared to be the perfect Savior through a continual, faithful, ordered prayer life, always reflecting the petitions of the Lord's Prayer. As he daily prayed to his Father in heaven, the various petitions would all eventually converge in a momentous way in Christ's passion narrative. And when you read the passion narrative, you can do so by reflecting on the Lord's Prayer and asking which petitions are being answered by his Father as our Lord goes to the cross, the supremely faithful one doing the will of God for the glory of his name in order to bring many sons to glory.

5

Jesus Prayed Joyfully in the Spirit

Luke 10:21

I thank you, Father, Lord of heaven and earth, that you have hidden these things from the wise and understanding and revealed them to little children; yes, Father, for such was your gracious will.

Jesus the Man of Joy

Christians must be joyful always (Phil. 4:4) and for good reasons. We should be joyful because of God's work in the salvation of sinners. And this work also includes the role of the Spirit in the life of God's people. Those in the Spirit necessarily respond to God's mighty acts of redemption, and never without joy.

The joy of Jesus exists as the foundation for our own. Throughout his Gospel, Luke clearly manifests the relationship between the Father and the Son, with the Holy Spirit acting as the bond of love and joy between them. What are the specific reasons for Christ's joy?

First, we must establish an important truth about the life of Christ on earth during his time of ministry when he faced many difficult challenges, culminating at the garden of Gethsemane and Golgotha. The Lord Jesus, while "a man of sorrows and acquainted with grief" (Isa. 53:3), always experienced joy. We might find this surprising until we realize a few important facts about Christian joy.

Christian joy is a fruit of the Spirit (Gal. 5:22; see also Acts 13:52). The possession of the Spirit implies the presence of his fruit in its entirety. A child of God may claim, "Well, I possess love but I do not have joy or self-control or patience." But our love is joyful love. Our patience is joyful patience. The fruit (singular in Gal. 5:22) of the Spirit means we must and will be truly (though imperfectly) loving, joyful, faithful, patient, and so on. In the case of our Lord, the man of the Spirit, he was filled with the Spirit beyond measure (John 3:34). In this manner, Christ possessed the fruit of the Spirit, including joy, fully and perfectly.

Anointed with the Spirit to accomplish his mission (Luke 3:21–22; 4:1, 14, 18), Jesus was necessarily filled with the Spirit of joy. In other words, if Jesus lacked joy, he would be devoid of love, and vice versa. This explains why he could have joy even in the time of supreme suffering (Heb. 12:2). No matter how intense his suffering was, Jesus knew there was a purpose in that suffering that would lead to his glory and ours.

Related to prayer specifically, Jesus in Luke 10:21 offers a prayer that begins with joyful thanksgiving. Gratitude toward

God always expresses itself in connection with a joyful heart. Psalms of thanksgiving abound, especially toward God for the works he has done. For example, Psalm 86:12–13:

> I give thanks to you, O Lord my God, with my whole
> heart,
>   and I will glorify your name forever.
> For great is your steadfast love toward me;
>   you have delivered my soul from the depths of Sheol.

And earlier in that same psalm,

> Gladden the soul of your servant,
>   for to you, O Lord, do I lift up my soul. (v. 4)

The psalm indicates that David faced many challenges in the "day" of his "trouble" (v. 7; see also vv. 1, 17). But thanksgiving to God for who he is and what he has promised to do is the handmaid of Christian joy. Without it, true thanksgiving disintegrates.

Jesus "rejoiced in the Holy Spirit" (Luke 10:21). Indeed, "rejoiced" is not quite strong enough; rather, the idea behind the Greek word is something akin to "exulted" or "jumped for joy." Prayer for him was joyful. This causes me a great deal of holy (I trust) envy of our Lord. Often, the last thing I feel like doing is praying. My sin hates communion with God. But Jesus, the sinless one, filled with the Spirit, had a joy in communion with God that we can both intensely desire and reverently admire. Truthfully, we can never utter to God a joyful word of thanksgiving apart from the Spirit. This was true for Christ and is certainly true for us. Joyful gratitude to God, when manifested in our lives, gives us confidence of the Spirit's work in us.

Joy Based on Truth

Rejoicing in the Holy Spirit expresses itself not merely as a feeling but as a feeling based on the truth. Jesus rejoiced in God's works, of which the Lord himself took part. As one who understood the mind of his Father in heaven, the Son could not refrain from rejoicing in the plan and works of the Father. Immediately after the short prayer in Luke 10:21, we read Jesus saying these words: "All things have been handed over to me by my Father, and no one knows who the Son is except the Father, or who the Father is except the Son and anyone to whom the Son chooses to reveal him" (v. 22).

Thus, when Jesus prayed these words, he completely understood them. He, unlike anyone else, saw the big picture, which acted as a catalyst for unbridled delight. Knowledge of the mind of God, illuminated by the Spirit, brings joy. Heaven will be a place of joy because we shall understand God in a manner this life does not allow. Jesus enjoyed knowledge of God's mind that encouraged rejoicing in him because our Lord knew that all would work out for God's glory and Christ's honor. In fact, willful ignorance is the friend of unhappiness; and Christ himself does not look approvingly upon those who pray with willful ignorance (Matt. 6:7).

In this prayer (Luke 10:21–22) Jesus rejoices in God's answer to the petition of the Lord's Prayer "your kingdom come." The growth of Christ's kingdom means the downfall of Satan's kingdom, just as the growth of holiness in our lives means the death of sin (Rom. 8:13). In Luke 10:17–18, we read of Satan's fall. We cannot know for sure when this happened, but ought to view it as the precursor to something greater in an "already–not yet," progressive unfolding of biblical redemptive history. The demons being subject to the seventy-two manifests Satan's fall

(v. 17); Christ's death is understood as a conquest over Satan (Heb. 2:14–15); and the return of Christ will usher in Satan's final, definitive defeat, when he shall be cast into the lake of fire (Rev. 20:10). The future destruction of Satan (not yet), which is guaranteed, had begun (already) with Christ's ministry on earth and the Spirit-filled power he delegated to his disciples (see Matt. 12:28).

What appears to be rather shocking was Christ's joy at God's blinding of learned and honored religious leaders ("the wise and understanding"). Jesus had already told the disciples to rejoice that their own names were written in heaven (Luke 10:20). They had to become like "little children" (Luke 10:21) in order to be written into the Lamb's Book of Life. "Little children" refers here to those who not only are dependent but also have no rights in and of themselves as commonly seen in first-century Roman culture. Jesus rejoiced that salvation came to such "nobodies," while the wise and learned, though honored in this life, had no time for the Lord and his redemption. Such an understanding of how God accomplishes his mighty acts of salvation brought Christ the type of joy that necessarily led to a natural outpouring of joyful prayer.

Joy in God's Will

In this prayer, Jesus focuses on the sovereign God, who as "Lord of heaven and earth" (Luke 10:21) actively accomplishes his will in everything, especially salvation. God reveals to some the saving truths of the gospel because he chose to do so. Many think it horrific that God could willfully reveal the gospel only to some while hiding it from others. Instead, Jesus sees this as a cause for thankful joy in his Father's gracious will.

Jesus essentially prays, "I heartily agree with how you do things," while affirming (in faith) and not questioning (in belief)

God's ways. Like Jesus, we cannot merely resign ourselves to but must actively and prayerfully rejoice in the accomplishment of God's sovereign will ("your will be done"), especially when it concerns his plan of saving the elect. Christ's prayer of thanksgiving rejoices in God's purposes, which ultimately get accomplished through him. Thus, his joy necessarily connects to not only what God does but also what he accomplishes through the death of Jesus, for which Jesus does in fact give thanks (Luke 22:17).

6

Jesus Prayed Knowing
He Would Be Heard

John 11:41–42

And Jesus lifted up his eyes and said, "Father, I thank you that you have heard me. I knew that you always hear me, but I said this on account of the people standing around, that they may believe that you sent me."

Not Always Heard

The Bible clearly teaches that sin can and does hinder prayer (Ps. 66:18; Prov. 28:9; Isa. 59:2; John 9:31; James 4:3; 1 Pet. 3:7). So, if sin creates a barrier between God and those praying, what about the opposite? John 9:31 answers this question when the man born blind attests the truth that "God does not listen to sinners, but if anyone is a worshiper of God and does his will, God listens to him." While the general truth applies to all worshipers, we must not miss the fact that the healed man in the immediate context was defending Jesus. In this way, the man was saying more than he realized. As the perfectly obedient worshiper (i.e., one who praised his Father), Jesus knew that "God listens to him" always.

Sometimes God does not hear his own people, his "treasured possession" (Deut. 7:6; 1 Pet. 2:9), when they pray. If they, either corporately or individually, are guilty of willful, perpetual sin, they can expect that these words in Isaiah 1:15 apply to them:

> When you spread out your hands,
> I will hide my eyes from you;
> even though you make many prayers,
> I will not listen;
> your hands are full of blood.

God's people have not always been heard by their covenant Lord. To whom much was given, much was expected. The rebellious Israelites could not presume that God would hear them always, no matter what they did or did not do. But in the case of our Lord Jesus, there was never any danger that his Father would say, "I will not listen; your hands are full of blood."

God Listens to Obedient Worshipers

When James speaks about the prayers of a "righteous" person having "great power" (James 5:16), he does not make an unconditional guarantee for every praying believer. While all Christians have access with confidence to the throne of grace (Heb. 4:15–16), James here likely attests to the unusual efficacy in the prayers of those who are peculiarly godly and have great faith.

Such people possess a gift for praying fervently and frequently. Not all Christians have the same gift for fervent prayer in the Spirit. If James did not mean that, he might have left out the mention of "a righteous person" and simply said, "Prayer has power." In short, godliness empowers prayer. Godliness entails a Christ-centered pursuit of all that God requires and an avoidance of all that he forbids.

James next mentions the example of the godly Elijah (James 5:17), whose fervent prayer accomplished great things. Elijah, in faith and according to God's will, earnestly prayed for rain to be withheld based on God's threats against his people, including the threat of drought (Deut. 28:22, 24). The prophet then prayed for rain to come based on God's promises of mercy. Of course, a righteous life entails much more than fervent prayer, but the two feed off one another. A godly life encourages us to be fervent in our petitions toward God. Our fervency toward him fosters godliness.

If Elijah provides such an example, how much more Jesus in his earthly prayers? Remember, he lived on earth as the man of prayer. Perfect in righteousness, he always prayed effectually as he lifted up his heart in faith fervently and frequently. Like Elijah, he also understood the will of God, yet without limitation.

Consider the apostle John's words: "And whatever we ask we receive from him, because we keep his commandments and do what pleases him" (1 John 3:22). This verse makes clear that receiving from God and obedience toward him go hand-in-hand. As Sinclair Ferguson notes: "This is why true prayer can never be divorced from real holiness. The prayer of faith can be made only by the 'righteous' man whose life is being more and more aligned with the covenant grace and purposes of God. In the realm of prayer, too . . . faith . . . without works . . . is dead."[1]

Jesus Was Heard by the Father

After Martha likely gave her consent—owing to some theological reasoning from Jesus—to have the stone removed from Lazarus's grave in John 11:38–40, Jesus offered a stunning prayer meant for the ears of his bystanders (John 11:41–42): "Father, I thank you that you have heard me. I knew that you always hear me, but I said this on account of the people standing around, that they may believe that you sent me." Jesus already expressed his confidence earlier, noting, "Our friend Lazarus has fallen asleep, but I go to awaken him" (John 11:11).

How could our Lord be so certain that his friend Lazarus would be raised from the dead? Was it because of the resurrection power he possessed (John 10:18)? For One who did only what the Father willed, such a use of divine power would seem presumptuous. Instead, the Spirit directed Jesus in the will of his Father concerning what he taught and what he did, including the miracle he would immediately perform. This indeed manifested Jesus's resurrection power, but he exercised it not of his own accord but in line with his Father's will (John 5:19). This perfect symmetry of purpose between the Son and the Father manifested the intimate relationship between the two; and, beautifully, the asking of the Son and the granting of the Father went together.

Still, we must not consider this simply as following out divine orders, especially given the relationship Jesus had with Lazarus. He was sad about his friend's death (John 11:35) yet knew that it would be the occasion for the glory of God (John 11:4). So Jesus in faith and with great confidence must have asked the

Father for the life of Lazarus. Where would such assurance come from? Simply, "the prayer of a righteous person has great power as it is working" (James 5:16).

Jesus asked and received because he asked in faith with no invisible barriers between himself and God. There existed no sin giving the Father grounds to turn a deaf ear. Because of Jesus's extraordinary person and life, the Father listened. So, even before the result came, our Lord amazingly expressed gratitude for answered prayer: "And Jesus lifted up his eyes and said, 'Father, I thank you that you have heard me. I knew that you always hear me'" (John 11:41–42).

In addition, we should not forget the words of Hebrews 5:7: "In the days of his flesh, Jesus offered up prayers and supplications, with loud cries and tears, to him who was able to save him from death, and he was heard because of his reverence." The righteousness of Christ remained instrumental to his prayers being heard, and such was manifested in his worshipful attitude of "reverence" (fear of God). Godly fear characterizes the soul of piety before God. As the person who knew God best, Jesus had a healthy fear of God that excelled all others'. That Jesus possessed an unparalleled earthly awareness of his Father made our Savior all the more worthy of answered prayer.

That Others May Know

Some theologians in history, especially when Arianism has posed a great threat to the church, have argued that Jesus merely prayed as a pattern for us to follow. Certain theologians have lacked clarity on whether Jesus needed to pray or he did so simply to show how prayer ought to be done. Some have used the Lazarus passage in this manner, where Jesus prayed, "But I said this on account of the people standing around, that they may believe that you sent me" (John 11:42).

But as noted above, Jesus had already petitioned the Father for Lazarus's life. He had prayed and received. He then thanked the Father for hearing him and allowed others a glimpse into this intimate relationship by praying audibly. So often in Christ's ministry he made it clear that he was no "lone ranger." Two or three witnesses attested everything he did. The primary witnesses in Christ's ministry were the Father and the Spirit. In his High Priestly Prayer in John 17, Jesus again desired that others know he was sent from the Father: "For I have given them the words that you gave me, and they have received them and have come to know in truth that I came from you; and they have believed that you sent me" (John 17:8). He prayed "that they may all be one, just as you, Father, are in me, and I in you, that they also may be in us, so that the world may believe that you have sent me" (John 17:21).

The entirety of Christ's ministry on earth vindicated that he came from Yahweh, Israel's God. The long-awaited Messiah ministered before God's people without hiding the fact that he came from the God of Abraham, Isaac, and Jacob. His miracles—such as the one performed in John 11—undeniably proved his claims. This was no imposter but God's faithful Son, always heard by the Father. Which, in our case as much as in Lazarus's, remains very good news indeed.

7

Jesus Prayed for His Father's Glory

John 12:27–28

"Now is my soul troubled. And what shall I say? 'Father, save me from this hour'? But for this purpose I have come to this hour. Father, glorify your name." Then a voice came from heaven: "I have glorified it, and I will glorify it again."

The Chief End of Christ

Many, even outside of the wider Presbyterian and Reformed tradition, know the first question and answer in the Westminster Shorter Catechism:

Q. 1. What is the chief end of man?
A. Man's chief end is to glorify God, and to enjoy him forever.

We are to glorify the One worthy of it (1 Cor. 10:31). Indeed, Christ's mission on earth perfectly sought to glorify his Father as his chief end: "I glorified you on earth, having accomplished the work that you gave me to do" (John 17:4). As a result of what Christ has done, I believe we can more fully suggest the following: *Our chief end is to glorify God (the Father) and Christ, through the Spirit, and enjoy them with God's people forever* (Rom. 11:36; 2 Cor. 13:14; Col. 1:16–18; Eph. 1:23; 3:16; Rev. 21:2).

We may continue this Trinitarian emphasis concerning Jesus: the Son glorified the Father through the Spirit and now enjoys the presence (i.e., the face) of God in heaven along with his redeemed people and the elect angels. But to have that vision of glory, and for us to be able to share in it, Jesus had to glorify the Father uniquely—through death.

A Troubled Soul

Christ informed his disciples of his troubled soul. As the Chalcedonian Creed makes clear, to be fully homoousios with humanity, the Son assumed a true human nature with both body and (a rational) soul.

Was Christ's soul troubled simply because he knew that his disciples would not remain faithful? This does not make sense of the words of John 12:27–28. Instead, we need to see his physical presence in Gethsemane as the culmination of the agony he endured throughout life as something of an "abiding Gethsemane." Now in that actual place, the realities of the cross hit him with full force. Here we encounter a particularly acute realization of his vicarious death on behalf of sinners, even before Golgotha.

In Psalm 6, David reveals the experiences of a troubled soul:

8

Be gracious to me, O Lord, for I am languishing;
  heal me, O Lord, for my bones are troubled.
My soul also is greatly troubled.
  But you, O Lord—how long?

Turn, O Lord, deliver my life;
  save me for the sake of your steadfast love.
For in death there is no remembrance of you;
  in Sheol who will give you praise? . . .

The Lord has heard my plea;
  the Lord accepts my prayer.
All my enemies shall be ashamed and greatly troubled;
  they shall turn back and be put to shame in a moment.
    (vv. 2–5, 9–10)

David prayed these words, but other godly people through the ages could also echo them, and they especially relate to Christ, whose troubled soul sought vindication.

Our Lord Jesus was no ghost whose docetic phantom without a true body or soul went through life without feeling or emotion. The verb translated "troubled" in John 12:27 here gives a sense of intensity and suggests horror. A deep vexation came over Christ concerning the cross. What did he do in such a time? He turned to theology and prayer.

What Shall I Say?

John describes here Christ's pre-Gethsemane "Gethsemane." Anticipating events near at hand, Jesus asks, "What shall I say?" Immediately following this question he appears to pray. He requests that the Father save him from "this hour" (John 12:27) probably not hypothetically with a question (as the ESV suggests), but with a simple petition as we see in Gethsemane: "And he said, 'Abba, Father, all things are possible for you. Remove this cup from me. Yet not what I will, but what you will'" (Mark 14:36).

What was at stake here? With his death coming soon, Christ knew what awaited him and expressed his pain to others not in weakness but with the strength that many in the church lack today. The "strong" do not tell others what bothers them, but such a tendency may manifest weakness and pride.

John Chrysostom (ca. 349–407) highlights Christ's troubles well:

> [This instance] greatly shows His humanity, and a nature unwilling to die, but clinging to the present life, proving that He was not exempt from human feelings. For as it is no blame to be hungry, or to sleep, so neither is it to desire the present life; and Christ indeed had a body pure from sin, yet not free from natural wants, for then it would not have been a body.[1]

What could Christ say? We can rightly understand his desire to be delivered from the horrendous hour that awaited him, a desire that manifested the necessary humanity of our Savior. Such remains as important as his divinity in securing our salvation.

Your Will Be Done

As Christ made a perpetual habit of doing the Father's will, he could pursue nothing else: "For I have come down from heaven, not to do my own will but the will of him who sent me" (John 6:38). Here he answers his own request for deliverance, as we often do while wrestling in prayer with some question, only to resolve it in the very act of prayer. Jesus essentially says, "Your will be done," recognizing, "for this purpose I have come to this hour." Obedience kisses death in this realization.

In this short prayer, we get great insight into the life of Jesus, which involved more than cruising along, performing miracles, feeding the hungry, and then unjustly receiving a death penalty at the hands of a kangaroo court. Much more.

We know that Jesus considered his death many times before this expression of anguish (e.g., Mark 8:31). Likewise, we have at least one other instance of Christ's troubled soul in Luke 12:50, where he speaks of his coming "baptism" (death) and how greatly it "distressed" or consumed him. In line with these examples, Isaiah speaks of Jesus as "a man of sorrows and acquainted with grief" (Isa. 53:3).

Glory Be to God the Father

Soli Deo gloria! To the glory of God alone. This Reformation "sola" easily falls off the lips of Protestants. But how many cry this out in the depths of despair? We know that seeking God's glory remains our "chief end," but at times we quickly turn to other solutions, seeking our own glory while running from the pain. When God puts our orthodox theology to the test in the troubles he providentially brings, he wants us to live out good theology, not simply know it. This was true for his Son; it will be true for us.

Jesus did this very thing as he primarily came to earth to glorify the Father: "The one who speaks on his own authority seeks his own glory; but the one who seeks the glory of him who sent him is true, and in him there is no falsehood" (John 7:18; see also 8:29, 50; 17:1, 4). How does one glorify God? Simply by obeying God's will revealed in Scriptures (Westminster Shorter Catechism, Q. 2). Jesus had a special command to obey beyond the required moral and ceremonial laws he observed. His Father required him to die on the cross.

When he resolved his "purpose" and desired to "glorify your [the Father's] name" ("your will be done" and "hallowed be your name"!), his Father answered with an audible voice, one of only three recorded instances during the ministry of Jesus when this took place. Speaking of his own name, the Father replied, "I have glorified and I will glorify it again," assuring his Son that the glory he sought would be secured without fail. We too lay hold of such a promise when we truly desire that God's name would be "hallowed" in life as well as in prayer. Like Christ, we can pray this prayer with assurance—"glorify your name."

8

Jesus Prayed for His Own Glory

John 17:1

*Father, the hour has come; glorify your
Son that the Son may glorify you.*

Heavenly Intercession

In this life, we will never fully appreciate the privilege of God speaking to us in Scripture. In Jesus's prayer in John 17, we get something beyond God's words to us, namely, a revelation into the inner sanctuary of the triune God. We have God (the Son) speaking to God (the Father) in the power of God (the Spirit). An abundance of great quotes from famous theologians tell of the glories of John 17. These can help us, but every Christian on his own, by the work of the Spirit, cannot help but marvel at the access God gives us here into the beauties and glories of the intra-Trinitarian relationship.

In the Gospel of John in general, and in this prayer particularly, we come across some dominating themes: obedience, glory, death, exaltation, discipleship, unity, and more. In general, we get here more extensive prayer content than in the Synoptic Gospels, as much as they do reference Christ's prayers (Matt. 6:9–13; 14:23; 19:13; 26:36–44; 27:46; Mark 1:35; 6:46; 14:32–39; 15:34; Luke 3:21; 5:16; 6:12; 9:18, 28–29; 11:1; 22:41–45; 23:46).

In many respects, John 17 provides a sacred body of divinity, teaching us much about God and doing so on holy ground. Many of the truths in John 17 are found scattered earlier in various forms throughout John's Gospel. Hints of Jesus's words and prayer come earlier, especially in John 12:27–28, but John 17 provides something so special that some advise us to simply read it over in reverent silence without comment. As compelling as this devotional counsel remains, we still do well to open and understand this prayer.

After the Upper Room Discourse, which may be the greatest sermon Christ ever offered his disciples, he prayed. Amazingly, in this prayer, we have a copy of this heavenly intercession. If you want to know how Christ currently intercedes for you with our Father in heaven, you can learn much from these words offered for your benefit while he was here on earth. Such petitions exist perpetually before the Father with no decrease ever in their power and efficacy. Their truths are, in a sense, reverberating around the heavenly places.

The Hour Came

Living, as he did, in a perpetual Gethsemane, Jesus always knew his "hour" would come. The plan eternally decreed became historically realized in our Lord's mind and heart. Up until that time, he and his ministry remained safe, with nothing to kill or even harm him. Why? His time had not yet come: "So they were seeking to arrest him, but no one laid a hand on him, because his hour had not yet come" (John 7:30; see also 7:6, 8; 8:20). Yet, when "some Greeks" came looking for Jesus (John 12:20–21), the hour arrived: "And Jesus answered them, 'The hour has come for the Son of Man to be glorified'" (John 12:23; see also 12:27–28, 31–32; 13:1, 31).

Jesus understood what this meant: "When I was with you day after day in the temple, you did not lay hands on me. But this is your hour, and the power of darkness" (Luke 22:53). Now, the forces of darkness would furiously come upon him. Despite the fact that his Father brought bitter punishment from the hands of men, Jesus still called upon him as Father. Christ understood that nothing calamitous could happen to him apart from the will of God. At the same time, he realized that he must confront the divinely appointed "calamity" when the time came.

This hour, when compared with eternity, lasted but a moment (Rom. 8:18), yet this did not minimize its agony (John 16:21). The way we should as God's children, the Son prayerfully cast himself upon God in this horrific situation. Strikingly, this prayer reveals Christ's supernatural knowledge of events yet to come. Judas and the other betrayers were nowhere to be seen at this point; and the Roman guards were not standing by with clubs and swords as Christ audibly proclaimed these words. Yet, Jesus knew that his hour had come. What a thought for him to endure. He knew that he, as the only truly innocent person in history, would be unjustly and publicly treated as a blaspheming criminal. Yet, he did not hide or wield divine power in defense.

He simply entrusted his heart, soul, mind, and strength to his Father in heaven.

Glory in Shame

As hideous as the cross was for Jesus, it provided the necessary way for his glorification (see John 13:31–33; Col. 1:16). Even in Christ's humiliation during his life on earth we detect hints of glory. The nature of the gospel and God's revelation to the world clearly manifest this.

For example, a baby placed in a lowly feeding trough (Luke 2:7) later receives worship from wise men guided by a glorious star (Matt. 2:1–2). Then, a soul assaulted by the furies of the Devil (Luke 4:1ff.) receives angelic assistance after his temptation (Matt. 4:11). Likewise, the Master denied the most basic hospitality by his prestigious dinner host receives glory from a prostitute tearfully wetting and kissing his feet (Luke 7:44–50). Or consider our crucified Savior, reviled by two criminals, receiving repentant and glorious worship from one of them.

Here are sparks of glory where there is shame.

Christ's humiliating death on the cross became part of his glory: "'Now is the judgment of this world; now will the ruler of this world be cast out. And I, when I am lifted up from the earth, will draw all people to myself.' He said this to show by what kind of death he was going to die" (John 12:31–33). In Christ's death, even before the resurrection, we see victory over the Devil (Gen. 3:15; Heb. 2:14). Here, he handled the sins of his people to his own glory in ignominy and to the doom of Satan. Christ did not go to the cross without knowing fully that his death would be his glory.

Note here that Christ alone could rightly be full of spiritual ambition, self-seeking, and desirous of glory, which remain based upon God's promises and declarations to Jesus: "How can you believe, when you receive glory from one another and do not seek the glory that comes from the only God?" (John 5:44). Like him, we should seek his glory, unlike the authorities in John 12 who "loved the glory that comes from man more than the glory that comes from God" (v. 43). The absence of promise implies the presence of presumption. We cannot expect to receive from God where there is not a promise to anchor the gifts given by him. As Thomas Manton (1620–1677) so appropriately says: "Here we may seek our own honour and glory without a crime. Oh! Behold the liberality and indulgence of grace! God has set no stint to our spiritual desires; we may seek not only grace, but glory."[1]

Yet, be warned, those who seek a worldly glory: God's glory given to us often comes wrapped in suffering. God makes us weak in order that we may be strong (2 Cor. 10). Christ did not escape the cross on his path to glory, and neither shall we. He prayed for glory, knowing that it comes only through the cross. Like Christ, we too must seek the glory that comes from God (Rom. 2:7).

Eternal Glory

The Father answered Christ's prayer for glory in what immediately followed, a glory *related to the great perspective of eternity*: he saved the church. In terms of Christ's public ministry on earth up to the point of his High Priestly Prayer, the words of the second servant song in Isaiah come to mind:

> But I said, "I have labored in vain;
>   I have spent my strength for nothing and vanity;
> yet surely my right is with the Lord,
>   and my recompense with my God." (Isa. 49:4)

Rejected by his own people and soon abandoned and denied by his disciples, Jesus might have concluded that he labored in vain. Yet he hoped not in people but in the Lord, who alone could give him his eternal and abundant reward for his humble obedience: "Therefore God has highly exalted him and bestowed on him the name that is above every name, so that at the name of Jesus every knee should bow, in heaven and on earth and under the earth, and every tongue confess that Jesus Christ is Lord, to the glory of God the Father" (Phil. 2:9–11). There exists no greater reward for the God-man, Jesus Christ, than this: lordship over all the created order. The Son will receive eternal worship in connection with a perpetual declaration of his lordship, cosmically and publicly.

Revelation, as challenging as it can be to interpret, clearly and abundantly manifests Christ's glory. The book of Revelation exists as an answer to Christ's prayer in John 17:1, "Glorify your Son." The events recorded here concerning the coming heaven on earth and our eternal dwellings on the new earth are all a reflection of the glory of Christ, of whom we read,

> Worthy is the Lamb who was slain,
> to receive power and wealth and wisdom and might
> and honor and glory and blessing! (Rev. 5:12)

What good news for those who know and love Christ, who shares his glory with us as his bride, the church. Christ is glorified in us and we in him (John 17:10). The more he receives, the more we receive. So praying "glorify your Son" makes sense not only for Christ but also for us. Desiring Christ's glory seeks our greatest spiritual benefit.

9

Jesus Prayed concerning Eternal Life

John 17:1–2

Father, the hour has come; glorify your Son that the Son may glorify you, since you have given him authority over all flesh, to give eternal life to all whom you have given him.

The Cross Glorifies the Father

In the context of Christ's priestly prayer, the Son's death at Calvary for sinners became his glory. In this way, the cross and Christ's glory revealed themselves as two sides of the same coin. As the Son received glory, so did the Father, the grand architect of this great redemption.

The Father nowhere, in all of creation and redemption, glorifies himself more than in his Son, Jesus Christ, the visible image of the invisible God (Col. 1:15), whose glory the face of Christ reveals (2 Cor. 4:6). In this life, for us, his "face" denotes not his physical visage but all that he represents and reveals concerning God in his earthly ministry, most specifically, his work on behalf of sinners. In the life to come, his "face" will be seen visibly and spiritually, giving us all of the knowledge of God and Christ that we could desire.

At the cross, the attributes of God shine more vividly and clearly than anywhere else in the Scriptures. God's wisdom, mercy, goodness, justice, grace, love, patience, wrath, and more are all set upon the hill at Golgotha when his beloved Son dies to save sinners. Through Christ, God shows himself to be both "just and the justifier of the one who has faith in Jesus" (Rom. 3:26). He shows his wisdom in defeating, through Jesus's weakness, the ruler of this world (Satan) (John 12:31; 2 Cor. 13:4; Heb. 2:14). Christ desired that his people should know God (John 17:3). So he went to the cross willingly, knowing that his death would glorify the Father by making his nature clear for all to see, know, and ultimately worship. As Calvin says:

> And God is glorified in him. This clause, which immediately follows the other, is added for confirmation; for it was a paradoxical statement, that the glory of the Son of man arose from a death which was reckoned ignominious among men, and was even accursed before God. He shows, therefore, in what manner he would obtain glory to himself from such a death. It is, because by it he glorifies God the Father; for in the cross of Christ:, as in a magnificent theater, the inestimable goodness of God is displayed before the whole world. In all the creatures, indeed, both high and low, the glory of God shines, but nowhere has it shone more brightly than in the cross, in which there has been an astonishing change of

things, the condemnation of all men has been manifested, sin has been blotted out, salvation has been restored to men; and, in short, the whole world has been renewed, and every thing restored to good order.[1]

Authority over All

The eternal, omnipotent, omniscient God does not receive authority; he possesses it infinitely and unchangeably by divine right. But in John 17:1–2 Jesus prays to his Father, acknowledging that his authority over all flesh comes from the Father. John (along with other Scripture passages) emphasizes this theme repeatedly:

- "The Father loves the Son and has given all things into his hand" (John 3:35).
- "All that the Father gives me will come to me, and whoever comes to me I will never cast out" (John 6:37).
- "And this is the will of him who sent me, that I should lose nothing of all that he has given me, but raise it up on the last day" (John 6:39).
- "My Father, who has given them to me, is greater than all, and no one is able to snatch them out of the Father's hand" (John 10:29).
- "Jesus, knowing that the Father had given all things into his hands, and that he had come from God and was going back to God . . ." (John 13:3).

What Christ prays for in John 17:1 concerning reciprocal glory between the Father and Son provides the ground for verse 2, where Jesus receives authority over all "flesh." This is a Semitic term, reminiscent of the language in Jeremiah 32:27: "Behold, I am the LORD, the God of all flesh. Is anything too hard for me?" Jesus takes these words to himself as the Savior of all flesh, for whom nothing is too hard. Because of his authority over all things, all whom the Father gives to Jesus will believe as his glory and reward. The Father gives to Jesus so that he (Jesus) may give to us.

So, after the resurrection, Jesus spoke to his disciples on a mountain where, upon seeing their Lord, they worshiped him. He then informed them, "All authority in heaven and on earth has been given to me" (Matt 28:18). As a result, they would succeed in their mission because Christ in his regal resurrection authority and power was sending them in the name of the triune God (Matt. 28:19–20). They would be the means by which God would grant to "all flesh" eternal life.

The Father granted to Jesus an authority of a mediatorial nature. His authority as the divine Son is equal to that of the other persons of the Trinity, but his prayer concerns his mediatorial authority as the God-man. Such comes as the result of Christ's faithfully finished and yet-to-be-applied work. The language concerning authority speaks of it as a reward belonging to Christ by way of a distinct and peculiar privilege.

Eternal Life

The Father committed all things to the Son. Christ's special knowledge of the Father was the ground for the Father allowing the Son to bring others into this knowledge of God (Matt. 11:27), which embodies eternal life as anticipated in the new covenant promises of Jeremiah 31:33–34:

> I will put my law within them, and I will write it on their hearts. And I will be their God, and they shall be my people. And no longer shall each one teach his neighbor and each his brother, saying, "Know the LORD," for they shall all know me, from the least of them to the greatest, declares the

LORD. For I will forgive their iniquity, and I will remember their sin no more.

Similarly, Paul considers the goal of his own "conversion experience" to be knowing Christ and the power of his resurrection (Phil. 3:10).

Christ described eternal life in terms of "knowing," because he possessed the mind of the Father, who committed all things to him. Christ alone knows the beauty and privilege of knowing God with a unique human knowledge sufficient for every human being everywhere for all eternity. From God's revelation to Christ emerges a desire, out of love and compassion, for others to share in his knowledge. For example, we see this in the Upper Room Discourse, where Jesus opens up such knowledge to his disciples for whom eternal life concerns knowing God and his Son. These blessings the Father gives his children through the Son and by the power of the Spirit cause us to rejoice with Daniel (Dan. 2:20–21).

Daniel answered and said:

> "Blessed be the name of God forever and ever,
>   to whom belong wisdom and might.
> He changes times and seasons;
>   he removes kings and sets up kings;
> he gives wisdom to the wise
>   and knowledge to those who have understanding."

Daniel desires to bless for eternity the name of God, who in his "wisdom and might" gives those he loves both wisdom and knowledge of himself. This beautifully describes the basic goal of eternal life.

The glory of eternal life concerns the privilege to know and so to love the triune God. All true knowledge of God results in our loving him. Now, salvation must include eternal life. Otherwise, what God gives would make us miserable, since it concerns only life temporally. Thus, a child of God possessing eternal life will know God more and more, forever. Still, in our ever-growing knowledge, we can never exhaust the glories of the triune God as the object of that knowledge.

10

Jesus Prayed for Us to Know God and Himself

John 17:3

And this is eternal life, that they know you, the only true God, and Jesus Christ whom you have sent.

The Only True God

Many people believe in, sacrifice much for, and devote themselves in service to "God." But they do so in vain if they fail to know the only true God, as Christ teaches us in John 17:3. Lack of knowledge destroys true religion, which God's people at times can be guilty of doing.

> Therefore my people go into exile
>   for lack of knowledge. (Isa. 5:13)

Yet this does not prevent God from accomplishing his ultimate purposes. The theme of God's glory and knowing him are brought together in Habakkuk 2:14:

> For the earth will be filled
>> with the knowledge of the glory of the LORD
>> as the waters cover the sea.

Knowledge of the only true God will fill the earth.

> But the LORD is the true God;
>> he is the living God and the everlasting King. (Jer. 10:10)

This basic Israelite confession expresses a conviction that one God exists, the one whom we serve. Since this one God reveals himself to humanity, he must demand absolute allegiance (1 Thess. 1:9).

Commenting on John 17:3, Calvin notes,

> Two epithets are added, true and only; because, in the first place, faith must distinguish God from the vain inventions of men, and embracing him with firm conviction, must never change or hesitate; and, secondly, believing that there is nothing defective or imperfect in God, faith must be satisfied with him alone.[1]

No faith survives except that which fixes itself upon the only true God. This faith must come as his gift (Eph. 2:8), which then leads us back to him. No other "god" could satisfy the faith that comes from the true and living God.

Yet Christ adds something here related to knowing God that seems unusual at first glance. He prays for people to know not only God but also "Jesus Christ," the one sent. Christ refers to himself in the third person here. We may not understand why he does this, but we must certainly find ourselves on the receiving end of this answered prayer.

We know the only true God only through Jesus Christ, our Mediator: "No one has ever seen God; the only God, who is at the Father's side, he has made him known" (John 1:18; see also Matt. 11:27). Jesus makes the Father known and provides the only way to him, even as he testifies: "I am the way, and the truth, and the life. No one comes to the Father except through me" (John 14:6). Not only does he make the Father "known," but he also makes the Father "knowable" in terms of approaching him. Every true believer must exercise such an approach.

Many, even in Jesus's day, claimed to believe in Yahweh, but Jesus demanded that such belief necessarily include faith in *him* as Yahweh. As God in the flesh, the second person of the blessed Trinity, he could not hide from people his true identity: "And Jesus cried out and said, 'Whoever believes in me, believes not in me but in him who sent me. And whoever sees me sees him who sent me'" (John 12:44–45).

Given the flow of Jesus's prayer so far in John 17, we find that the significance of saving knowledge of God and Christ concerns the glory the created world is designed to give him. God created the world to glorify himself. In this, the Father, by the Spirit, brings glory to the God-man (his Son), whose aim is to glorify the Father, which he does in the power of the Spirit. Arguing for any way to God other than through Jesus Christ would derogate the glory of God, since that is principally how God glorifies himself.

Knowing the Father

In the prayer of John 17:3, Jesus asks that those receiving eternal life know the only true God. Does he refer to the Father, Son, and

Holy Spirit here? Yes and no. They are all coequal; there is one God. But then our Lord also adds, "and Jesus Christ whom you have sent" (John 17:3). This language solves the problem for us.

Certain outward works—depending on what they are—are more peculiarly attributed to one or another of the three persons of the Godhead. This is known as the doctrine of appropriations. All the persons share a common prerogative. However, for example, a work may be attributed to the Father in order to display his uniqueness in the order of persons (e.g., reconciliation is to the Father—2 Cor. 5:18–19). The triune God's undivided outward works (*ad extra*) often reveal specifically one of the persons (as a terminal work), even though the outward works of the triune God are nevertheless undivided.

In the order and economy of God's redemptive work, the Father sends the Son, who willingly goes as the Father's Son and representative (John 3:17; 17:18; 20:21; Gal. 4:4). The New Testament commonly refers to the Father simply as "God" and at times clearly distinguishes between God (the Father) and Christ. This is "economical" language, found, for example, in 1 Corinthians 8:6: "Yet for us there is one God, the Father, from whom are all things and for whom we exist, and one Lord, Jesus Christ, through whom are all things and through whom we exist" (see also 1 Cor. 15:15, 27; 2 Cor. 13:14).

In the New Testament, following the principle spoken of above, we find that God and Christ are differentiated as distinct persons. The New Testament informs us that it is the Father to whom reconciliation, through Christ, is made (2 Cor. 5:18–19). The Father is first in the order of subsistence, so in the economy of salvation the Son reconciles us to the Father. We should note, of course, that reconciliation involves more than having our sins forgiven, as it expresses in a fuller sense the reality that the Son brings us to the Father for communion (i.e., to know him).

As John Owen noted so well in his somewhat groundbreaking work *On Communion with God* (vol. 2 in his *Works*), believers commune with the Father principally in love. Jesus prays that we may know the Father, which denotes loving the Father and knowing his love for us. Knowing the Father, for Owen, means endearing our souls to him so that we delight in him. Yet Owen laments—and this may be applied to many of us in the church today (regrettably)—that many Christians do not delight and rejoice in God their Father as they should:

> There is still an indisposedness of spirit unto close walking with him. What is at the bottom of this distemper? Is it not their unskillfulness in or neglect of this duty, even of holding communion with the Father in love? So much as we see of the love of God, so much shall we delight in him, and no more. Every other discovery of God, without this, will but make the soul fly from him; but if the heart be once much taken up with this the eminency of the Father's love, it cannot choose but be overpowered, conquered, and endeared unto him. This, if any thing, will work upon us to make our abode with him. If the love of a father will not make a child delight in him, what will?[2]

All true knowledge of God involves mutual loving discourse between God and the redeemed sinner. Love desires knowledge of the person loved. God knows us perfectly, and we must, with all the assistance he affords us, aim to know him. If this were not supremely important, Christ would not have highlighted this so often in his ministry and specifically in this prayer.

Knowing Christ

Peter knew Christ while and after the Lord lived on this earth. Peter had this distinct privilege as an intimate disciple and apostle. Years after Christ's ascension, and with apostolic authority, Peter commanded believers to "grow in the grace and knowledge of our Lord and Savior Jesus Christ. To him be the glory both now and to the day of eternity. Amen" (2 Pet. 3:18). Again, we see the themes of Christ's glory and the knowledge of him tied together. The more we come to know him, the more he receives glory. What Jesus prayed for, Peter commanded on Christ's behalf. One wonders if Christ's High Priestly Prayer flashed through Peter's mind when he gave this rousing benediction. Whatever the case, knowing Christ in his person and work is not optional for a Christian. Instead, it remains for us a dutiful delight.

Jesus, if he were not the God-man "in whom are hidden all the treasures of wisdom and knowledge" (Col. 2:3), would sound like a madman in this prayer. Jesus wants people—"a great multitude that no one could number, from every nation, from all tribes and peoples and languages" (Rev. 7:9)—to know him. Either he must be worth knowing or the Jews were correct to accuse him of blasphemy.

Of course he *is* worth knowing, and knowing well. He is "the Son of the living God" (Matt. 16:16); the Word who became flesh (John 1:14); "the image of the invisible God" (Col. 1:15); "the radiance of the glory of God" (Heb. 1:3); "the King, the LORD of hosts" (Isa. 6:5); and the One to whom "every knee [will] bow, in heaven and on the earth and under the earth," acknowledging that he "is Lord, to the glory of God the Father" (Phil. 2:10–11). If the world itself cannot "contain the books that would be written" about the man Christ Jesus, then he is someone worth knowing (John 21:25).

His prayer concerning eternal life shows us that Christianity concerns so much more than having a "get out of jail [i.e., hell] free card." The Christian life is not primarily something negative (what we have been saved from) but positive (whom we have been saved to). We are saved in order to know God and Christ, to live in communion with them for eternity. To know that the Father sent his best (the Son) for the worst (sinners) should provide great impetus for us to know more of this God filled with mercy, grace, wisdom, and truth. By knowing Christ we know God, and by knowing God we know Christ.

Jesus Prayed for the Glory He Had Before the World Existed

John 17:4–5

I glorified you on earth, having accomplished the work that you gave me to do. And now, Father, glorify me in your own presence with the glory that I had with you before the world existed.

Doing the Father's Will

The Father sent the Son into the world to do a great work. Most importantly, he came to do the Father's will in order to glorify him and thereby receive his own peculiar reward of glory. The Father did not create a world for any higher end than that he would be glorified by his creation. Jesus offers to God the highest instance of glory. But in doing so he possesses his own unique glory.

In spite of the disobedience our infinite God as Creator would endure from his finite creatures from the time of Adam and Eve in the garden of Eden until the coming final judgment, he did not immediately destroy the world. Such a wait was justified because of the obedience and work that God had given Jesus Christ to do.

In Isaiah's third servant song we read of the obedience of God's servant:

> The Lord God has opened my ear,
>> and I was not rebellious;
>> I turned not backward.
> I gave my back to those who strike,
>> and my cheeks to those who pull out the beard;
> I hid not my face
>> from disgrace and spitting. (Isa. 50:5–6)

The Father gave the servant (Christ) a painful and humiliating work, which was appreciated by very few during his life. But Jesus knew well the arduous task he took upon himself and willingly did it with the resolution, "My food is to do the will of him who sent me and to accomplish his work" (John 4:34; see also 5:36).

Jesus also knew that his work was not in vain. At times we can understand why Jesus may have cried,

> But I said, "I have labored in vain;
>> I have spent my strength for nothing and vanity."
>> (Isa. 49:4)

After all, even when many believed in Jesus, he did "not entrust himself to them because he knew all people and needed no one to bear witness about man, for he himself knew what was in man" (John 2:23–25). Far from being overly cynical, Jesus was ultimately vindicated many times over the course of his ministry (see John 6:66). Because he remained so firmly fixed upon doing the Father's will, he knew that his work would not ultimately be in vain. Hence, God's response to the servant in Isaiah 49:

> It is too light a thing that you should be my servant
> > to raise up the tribes of Jacob
> > and to bring back the preserved of Israel;
> I will make you as a light for the nations,
> > that my salvation may reach to the end of the earth.
> > (v. 6)

As he prayed the prayer of John 17, Jesus knew that completing the Father's work would bring him a great reward. He would become a "light for the nations." Obviously, at this point, Jesus had not yet completed his mission. Yet he spoke here in a proleptic manner, as if his future work were already accomplished. This prayer before the "it is finished" work of the cross treated his mission as "good as done," as we sometimes say. For even the greatest saint today, such praying would be presumption, but not for the sinless Son of God. He had all his life obeyed the Father perfectly, completely, and joyfully. He possessed every right at this point to speak as though the work had been completed. As such, he asked for his reward: glory.

The Glory before the World Existed

God does not give his glory to anyone (Isa. 42:8), which all Israelites understood. Jesus from his own knowledge and the synagogue readings from the Old Testament Scriptures during his youth knew this quite well. All that God does is for himself.

For my own sake, for my own sake, I do it,
> for how should my name be profaned?
> My glory I will not give to another. (Isa. 48:11)

If Jesus were not God, his praying for his own glory would have reeked of heresy and blasphemy. He would have been asking for something, as a student of the Old Testament Scriptures, without any right to do so. Yet he requested a glory he in fact had with the Father before the creation of the world. Jesus knew not only his entitlement to this glory but also that it made sense if he was the preexistent Son of God. However, there remain some interpretative difficulties for us to address in this passage.

Because of the historical reality of the Son assuming a true human nature (not a human person), how could he ask for something he possessed before the foundation of the world (and thus before the incarnation)? Was Christ speaking according to his divine nature or his human nature? If the former, how could God's glory, which is infinite, unchangeable, and eternal, be in any way diminished or lost so that it had to be recovered or given? Yet, if he was speaking of his human nature, how could he receive something granted in eternity past, since the Son became flesh in time (i.e., the incarnation was a real historical event)?

First, Christ asked as the Mediator, the God-man. He requested glory as a person, not as a human or divine nature. Some say that Christ petitioned for the glory belonging to the second person of the Trinity, God the Son. Others maintain that a supposed restoration of glory to any person of the Trinity could not happen, since it could not be lessened in the first place. God's glory cannot be diminished, any more than an attribute of his can be diminished. God is unchangeable and infinite in all his attributes.

Christ requested a glory that was veiled or suspended during his time on earth. Hence, this particular glory could not be naked divine glory. It had to be something else. Thomas Goodwin (1600–1680) offers perhaps the most satisfying treatment on this matter. He denies that the Son's former glory before the world existed refers to what was his as God the Son, simply considered in his divinity. It was the personal glory of the God-man, Jesus Christ.

As God, the Son did not need to pray for glory. In fact, even while he was on earth, the Son remained fully God and thus totally glorious. Since he did ask for a glory, there must have been a "suspension" (so Goodwin) of that glory, which he had before the creation of the world. Hence, as Goodwin notes, the "subject of the glory prayed for is the man. . . . Now, that it is the man, or rather the person of the God-man in union together, is the subject prayed for, is evident" for the following reasons:

1. Christ prayed as one humiliated but nonetheless faithful in his work for the Father.
2. While the glory he requested had been suspended, it remained a certain reward: "Was it not necessary that the Christ should suffer these things and enter into his glory?" (Luke 24:26).
3. He sought a heavenly glory that would appear in his human nature as the eternal God-man. This is the glory he desired his people to see: "Father, I desire that they also, whom you have given me, may be with me where I am, to see my glory that you have given me because you loved me before the foundation of the world" (John 17:24).
4. John 17:24 refers to a glory given to Christ that redeemed saints also can enjoy. Even in our own glorification, we shall not be able to apprehend the essential

glory of God. It must be mediated through his Son, Jesus Christ.

5. God is a Spirit, and so we who are human beings see God visibly in the face of Jesus Christ. Seeing is both ocular and intellectual, which requires God's condescension toward (even exalted) human beings.

So how could Christ have a glory before the creation of the world? Goodwin answers:

> It was the glory which the second person, being in God's singular predestination of him constituted God-man, had in and by the same predestination given him, as the glory of the only begotten Son of God, as his due in the perfect and exquisite idea thereof, then given him, and pre-ordained unto him.[1]

Augustine basically offered the same interpretation, even though he was fighting the Arians and had every reason to affirm the other view mentioned above. Goodwin continues, "God having first, and with a primary chief intendment, estated Christ absolutely, singly, independently, in his personal glory, and in his predestination of him, God-man, gave him that original as the grand lease of all creature glory" (1 Cor. 2:8).[2]

John Owen also takes this view:

> But there was a peculiar glory and honour belonging unto the person of the Son, as designed by the Father unto the execution of all the counsels of his will. Hence was that prayer of his upon the accomplishment of them: (John 17:5:) "And now, O Father, glorify me with thine own self, with the glory which I had with thee before the world was." To suppose that the Lord Christ prays, in these words, for such a real communication of the properties of the divine nature

unto the human as should render it immense, omniscient, and unconfined unto any space—is to think that he prayed for the destruction, and not the exaltation of it.[3]

God the Father blessed the Son as the Mediator of the elect with a predestined glory that included his promised reward for faithful accomplishment of his work. The glory promised to him included being the Head of the church, Savior of the world, and visible image of God crowned with glory and honor.

God gave this glory to Christ, then, at the very moment that God predestined him to it, even though it was obscured to men in his state of humiliation. Because the Son was a preexistent person, this was not only possible but also suitable to God's grand design and purposes. The Son knew before the foundation of the world the glory that would be his as Mediator. He voluntarily entered into this world of sin and misery, knowing that he alone would redeem the world from its present state of bondage and decay. Rightly, then, he asked for his glory as the One who would fulfill the preordained purposes of God.

We can and must pray for those things that have been given to us from before the creation of the world. God has blessed us in eternity with all spiritual blessings in Christ, including a conformity to his image (Rom. 8:29). We can pray, "Father, glorify us, by making us like your Son in this life by faith and in the life to come by sight." We possessed this glory when we were chosen in Christ (Eph. 1:4–5), but the fulfillment of this glory, which is ours, since we are raised with him already (Col. 3:1), is still to come. Until then, we must pray for this reality to take place.

12

Jesus Prayed concerning God's Self-Disclosure

John 17:6–8

I have manifested your name to the people whom you gave me out of the world. Yours they were, and you gave them to me, and they have kept your word. Now they know that everything that you have given me is from you. For I have given them the words that you gave me, and they have received them and have come to know in truth that I came from you; and they have believed that you sent me.

Christ, the Sacred Repository

One of the most important yet often unnoticed aspects of our salvation concerns the fact that Jesus is the "repository" (i.e., source, fountain) of all saving truth that God reveals to the church. Jesus not only is the repository but also provides the sum and focus of all divine revealed truth. Since he is God incarnate, there is no theology without Christ. Paul's desire for the church in Colossae was for their hearts to be encouraged, to be joined together in love, and "to reach all the riches of full assurance of understanding and the knowledge of God's mystery, which is Christ, in whom are hidden all the treasures of wisdom and knowledge" (Col. 2:2–3).

As the God-man, the only Mediator between God and the elect, Jesus communicates all of God's gospel mysteries to the church. Stephen Charnock (1628–1680) observes, "Whatsoever tends to the glory of God . . . is fully revealed by Christ."[1] The Son knows the Father and so reveals him. No sinful human being could do this of himself. Christ possesses an intimacy with the Father and Spirit that no mere man could understand, expect, or claim (John 3:13). In addition, Christ was the "medium of the first discovery of God in the creation" (see Prov. 8:22; John 1:3–4; Heb. 1:2). Christ is the wisdom and power of God, not only in creation, but also in redemption.

Charnock adds:

Now, as in the creation the Son communicated to all creatures some resemblance of God, and the end of the creation being to declare God to the rational creature, it was most proper for the Son of God to make those further declarations of him which were necessary, who at first made the manifestation of God in the frame of the world. As the beautiful image of reason in the mind, breaking out with the discovery of itself in speech and words, is fittest to express the inward sense, thoughts, conceptions, nature, and posture of the mind, so the essential Word of God clothes himself with flesh, comes out from God to manifest to us the nature and thoughts of God. He which is the word of God is fittest to manifest the nature of God.[2]

Only Christ could perfectly manifest God's name (i.e., his being). Hence, the "great end" of the Son's coming into the world, when sent by the Father in the power of the Spirit, was to reveal God (Matt. 13:35; John 1:18). Whatever content we find in the Scriptures, it is from the hand of Christ. Indeed, red-letter Bibles miss an important theological point, namely, that all of the words are Christ's.

So important is Christ to the idea of God's revelation that even the angels depend on their knowledge of God from Christ, the instrument of the angels' very creation. According to Charnock, as the angels looked upon the life of Christ unfolding during his public ministry on earth, particularly the last days and hours, "they learned more of God and his nature, more of the depths of his wisdom, treasures of his grace, and power of his wrath, than they had done by all God's actions in the world . . . in all those four thousand years wherein they had remained in being."[3]

Manifestation of God's Name

One of the principal ends of Christ's ministry on earth concerned manifesting God's name. In prayer, he rightly told the Father what he already knew. God already knows all we tell him. So prayer involves more than simply telling him something he already knows. Christ confirmed the truth in prayer.

In John 6:45–46, Christ begins answering his critics by quoting from Isaiah 54:13, "All your children shall be taught by the Lord." Those who belong to Yahweh will belong to Christ, for he operates as the mouthpiece of Yahweh. He mediates all knowledge of Yahweh to those the Father gives him: "Everyone who has heard and learned from the Father comes to me" (John 6:45).

Out of John 17:6–8 comes confidence in Christ's ministry. He has faithfully revealed the Father, which only Christ can do, having seen the Father (John 6:46). Whether in his works or in his words, Jesus reveals the name of the Father. This "name" (John 17:6) entails much more than a mere name and extends to all God reveals to us about himself. Why should people believe that Jesus comes from the Father? Because they belong to the Father and Jesus is begotten of the Father, all who claim to know God can do so only through Jesus Christ. When people heard Jesus speak, they also heard the Father speaking through him, for Jesus's words came from the Father (John 17:8).

We should remember the joy this must have brought Christ as he prayed these words. The principal mouthpiece of God, he was made privy to the Father's will. Thus, he possessed the singular privilege of knowing the Father in a way that made him alone fit to reveal the secrets of the kingdom (Matt. 13:11). All of Christ's words are God's words (John 5:19–30), which remains fitting for the One called the Word (John 1:1, 14).

Concerning God's People

Christ's confidence in prayer arose out of the natural relationship he possesses with the Father. Moreover, he prayed in the Spirit, according to the will of God. In this respect, according to God's will, Christ entered the world as a representative for the people God gave him. Psalm 2:8 makes this clear:

> Ask of me, and I will make the nations your heritage,
>> and the ends of the earth your possession.

John had earlier stated this truth about Christ explicitly: "All that the Father gives me will come to me, and whoever comes to me I will never cast out" (John 6:37; see also 10:28–29). Jesus reveals himself in a unique manner to those the Father gives him. Our Lord here prayed based upon God's promise, with a confidence that such promises are "Yes" and "Amen" in Christ (2 Cor. 1:20).

One of the most important desires for Christ as God's Messiah was for people to recognize him simply as that: Yahweh's servant/Messiah. Sent from God as Mediator on our behalf, Jesus prayed concerning this matter because, ultimately, it remains the great end of our salvation, namely, coming to know God and Christ (John 17:3).

In John 17:6–8 Jesus commends his people to his Father just as he had commended his Father to his people. There will never be a break in the chain between God's people and himself, since Christ and the Spirit are the bonds keeping us in God's favor and love forever. What Jesus says here must be true of every true child of God. Each one receives and keeps God's Word because it comes from the hand of Christ, who himself gives us his Spirit, that we will believe the things of God.

Remarkably, Christ pleads our case in this manner to the Father. Could he not have said, "They have barely kept your word; they have disbelieved the promises of God; they are slow and dull of hearing"? Instead, despite the many weaknesses and failings of God's people, Christ still commends us. This should give us confidence now that while Christ intercedes in heaven, he manifests more interest in bringing to the Father our obedience than in bringing our disobedience. As a pleased Savior he looks down upon us with confidence that his power and work in us will please the Father. Why? Because the Father must be pleased with his Son's work.

Keeping the Words of God

Words that testify to Christ are of paramount importance. We cannot be tentative about this matter. Hence Christ made it his aim in his prayer to confirm the truth that his people keep God's Word. The Scripture clearly expresses the reality of and need for such faithful adherence:

- "But [Jesus] said, 'Blessed rather are those who hear the word of God and keep it!'" (Luke 11:28).
- "But [Jesus] answered them, 'My mother and my brothers are those who hear the word of God and do it'" (Luke 8:21).
- "But be doers of the word, and not hearers only, deceiving yourselves" (James 1:22).

Clearly God demands that hearing must lead to doing. Such will be fulfilled in all whom the Father gives to the Son. Christ's prayer in this instance will certainly accomplish this. Our zeal for keeping God's Word results from how we receive it when it is preached (see 1 Thess. 2:13). Receiving the Word from the hands of Christ himself, who assures us of our great salvation, will surely lead to obedience. That we keep the Word is really a blessing of our salvation that Christ prays about. Thus, Christ prays concerning our whole salvation, not just a part.

Are we to keep God's Word? Yes. Will we keep God's Word? Yes, truly, albeit imperfectly in this life. Christ made this possible by praying with this aim in mind. If you are a Christian and keep God's Word, take heart that Christ prayed for you to do so. The Father gave you to Christ, who kept God's Word and prayed to the Father for your ability to "hear" and "do" in a way that accomplishes God's purposes. All of our obedience (in the power of the Spirit) comes as an answer to the Son's prayer. What a humbling yet comforting reality!

13

Jesus Prayed for the Elect to Glorify Him

John 17:9–10

I am praying for them. I am not praying for the world but for those whom you have given me, for they are yours. All mine are yours, and yours are mine, and I am glorified in them.

Christ Prays Not for the World

Very simply, Christ saves those for whom he intercedes. If he prayed, according to God's will, for the whole world to be saved, then every individual without exception would be saved. Yet he does not do that, as we see in John 17:9–10. He prays to his Father not "for the world, but for those you have given me." He intercedes for those elected to salvation according to the Father's sovereign plan. As Thomas Manton observes (quoting John Cameron and John Owen), "We must distinguish the prayers of Christ as a holy man, and the prayers of Christ as mediator."[1] As a holy man, Christ needed to pray for his enemies (Matt. 5:44). However, as a Mediator, he prayed only for the elect, as is the case in John 17.

Not all have agreed with this understanding of John 17. Many suggest that Jesus prayed for his apostles here in order that they would take the word to the world. However, as D. A. Carson notes, the distinction Christ makes is not merely utilitarian, as if Jesus only prayed for his disciples to bring the word to the world. Carson explains:

> True, their mission is mentioned a few verses later (v. 18), and Jesus can pray for those who will believe in him through their message (v. 20). Even so, the fundamental reason for Jesus' self-imposed restriction as to whom he prays for at this point is not utilitarian or missiological but theological: *they are yours*. However wide is the love of God (3:16), however salvific the stance of Jesus toward the world (12:47), there is a peculiar relationship of love, intimacy, disclosure, obedience, faith, dependence, joy, peace, eschatological blessing and fruitfulness that binds the disciples together and with the Godhead.[2]

The immediate context of the prayer shows us that, while the apostles may be chiefly in view, they are not exclusively so. The Father gives all things to his Son (John 5:19–24). Here Christ reminds his Father of their common interest in the people given by the Father. They were chosen, in Christ, by the Father (Eph. 1:3–5). Christ prays as Mediator for those given, which includes not just his core group of word-bearing disciples but also all the elect everywhere for all times to come.

Notice, as well, that the language of Christ's prayer is too intimate for those who reject him. Christ's intercession without fail efficaciously results in the salvation of anyone for whom he prays. In short, Christ does not intercede for those not given to him, the reprobate.

The Nature of Christ's Intercession

The Westminster Shorter Catechism states concerning Christ's mediatorial priesthood, "Christ executes the office of a priest, in his once offering up of himself a sacrifice to satisfy divine justice, and reconcile us to God, and in making continual intercession for us" (Q. 25). Reformed theologians have commonly treated Christ's priesthood in terms of oblation (the sacrifice offered) and intercession. As Charnock notes, "They are both joined together, but one as precedent to the other. . . . The oblation precedes the intercession, and the intercession could not be without the oblation."[3]

John Owen also speaks to this aspect of Christ's mediatorial work: "It belongs to the same mediator for sin to sacrifice and pray."[4] As noted already, the prayer in John 17 functions as a type of his prayer in heaven. Christ's earthly prayer here prefigures his heavenly intercession. Moreover, in heaven, Christ's intercessory work functions as a continued oblation. In other words, according to Owen, "whatsoever Christ impetrated [entreated], merited, or obtained by his death and passion, must be infallibly applied unto and bestowed upon them for whom he intended to obtain it; or else his intercession is vain, he is not heard in the prayers of his mediatorship."[5]

In his office as priest, Christ's sacrificial death (oblation) and intercession join together inseparably. Manton explains that the Old Testament high priest "entered [the Most Holy Place] not for himself, but for the people, having the names of the twelve tribes upon his breast and shoulders; so Christ is entered on behalf of us all, bearing the particular memorial of every saint graven on his heart."[6]

The Fruits of Christ's Intercession

In heaven, our Lord applies the benefits of his life and death to the church that he purchased with his blood (Acts 20:28). Historically, many Reformed theologians contended that the full justification of the elect depends, in the final analysis, on Christ's intercession. Thomas Watson (1620–1686) says, for example, "But [from where] is it that we are justified? It is from Christ's intercession."[7]

In Christ's death, he procures or obtains our forgiveness. But his intercession is the means by which his death's merits are applied to us. If Christ dies for someone, he will certainly intercede for that person. The Father cannot deny such a request. He will not turn away those for whom Christ intercedes.

Now, in relation to what Christ prays here (John 17:9–10), we see that Christ is glorified in those given by the Father. Christ prays for those who will glorify him. This helps us to understand the scope of Christ's prayer here. He prays for all those who bring him glory.

For Christ to be glorified in his people, there will be certain marks among his people. First, we will be justified by his blood and given the right to eternal glory. We will be saved apart from works because of the works of the God-man. Second, we will be given new life, changed from a state of wrath to a state of grace, which includes godliness (Christlike conformity).

As we read in 2 Peter 1:3–4,

> His divine power has granted to us all things that pertain to life and godliness, through the knowledge of him who called us to his own glory and excellence, by which he has granted

to us his precious and very great promises, so that through them you may become partakers of the divine nature, having escaped from the corruption that is in the world because of sinful desire.

Third, to glorify him on earth signifies our future heavenly glorification of him. We glorify him now not only in our holiness (2 Cor. 3:18) but also in our suffering (2 Tim. 2:12). Eternity, then, will be a continuation of what happened in our hearts and on our lips here on earth (Rom. 15:6–7; Rev. 1:6; 5:12–13). Why do some possess a burning love for Christ and long for his appearance (1 Pet. 1:7–8)? Because Christ prayed that he would be glorified in us (John 17:10).

Christ possesses a natural glory as very God of very God. He also possesses a peculiar glory as the God-man, the visible image of the invisible God. But besides those two glories, he possesses a third glory: the glory that comes to him from his bride. This depends not upon us (part of his creation), in the final analysis. The glory certainly comes to him through us because he prayed for us to bring glory to him.

When we understand John 17:9 in its immediate context, we see clearly that those who glorify Christ are those for whom he prays, those given by the Father. The faith given to us from above is supernatural faith and will bring forth praises that speak of the Son's great name—the name above every name (Phil. 2:11).

We should be rather amazed at the thought that we glorify Christ. But, as Paul says in Ephesians 1:22–23, the church is his body, "the fullness of him who fills all in all." We are Christ's fullness in the sense that he is our Husband and we, as his bride, complete him. In the way that God has planned salvation, the bride and Bridegroom rightly and wonderfully complement each other. No wonder, then, that Christ makes this a burden in his prayer. He established in his familiar conversation with his Father in John 17 something he has been saying ever since: "I am glorified in them" (v. 10). God the Father, God the Son, and God the Holy Spirit—all one God—will make sure that the church glorifies Christ.

Manton wonderfully notes that Jesus "is interceding for you in heaven when you are glorifying him on earth; he is doing your business in heaven when you are doing his business in the world."[8] Mutual reciprocal love manifests itself when Christ takes care of us from his heavenly throne as Intercessor, and we take care to honor and glorify him on earth.

We behave like the Father when we glorify the Son. Manton adds: "God's great end in all his dispensations is to glorify his Son, and in his Son himself; God seeks his own glory by glorifying Christ in our nature. We had neither had word, nor gospel, nor Christ, nor grace, but for his glory."[9]

14

Jesus Prayed That the Father Would Protect the Church

John 17:11–12

And I am no longer in the world, but they are in the world, and I am coming to you. Holy Father, keep them in your name, which you have given me, that they may be one, even as we are one. While I was with them, I kept them in your name, which you have given me. I have guarded them, and not one of them has been lost except the son of destruction, that the Scripture might be fulfilled.

The Beginning of Intercession

Jesus prayed in John 17:11, "Holy Father, keep them in your name." It naturally follows from verse 10 that we need protection from the forces of evil in order to glorify the Son as he declared we would. Our Lord understood that his time on earth was coming to an end, while his followers would remain in the world. Christ's gain was obvious: he was to be seated in glory at the right hand of his Father ("I am coming to you").

Christ's ascension does not usually receive the attention it deserves. The cross and his resurrection from the dead were not his only triumphs. His victories, if we may put it that way, continued and will continue. We must not miss the bursting joy he experienced in anticipation of his return to the Father's presence. The New Testament carefully highlights the fact that Jesus, as the God-man, not just as a free-floating soul, ascended into the heavenly places (Acts 1:9–11).

As Christ studied the Old Testament Scriptures during his life, he would have come to realize that one day he would be seated in glory on a throne in heaven.

> The LORD says to my Lord:
>   "Sit at my right hand,
> until I make your enemies your footstool." (Ps. 110:1)

Christ, after defeating the Devil on the cross, rising from the dead, and spending forty days on earth, not only ascended into heaven as a triumphant conqueror and God's beloved Son; he also knew that he would be taking the requests of this prayer with him into heaven as he continued his ministry as our Prophet, Priest, and King. So, when he prayed, "I am coming to you," his continuing work for the objects of his current intercession was implied.

Keep Them

The unique approach of Jesus in this prayer, "Holy Father," occurs nowhere else in the Bible. Intimate, yet transcendent, Jesus approached his Father with reverence (Heb. 5:7). He knew a petition characterized by such would be heard. What is the precise nature of that request?

Christ's words "keep them in your name" have been variously understood. Some argue that Christ here asks for his followers to be kept by the power of God's name, an idea with rich Old Testament connections. For example,

> The name of the LORD is a strong tower;
>> the righteous man runs into it and is safe. (Prov. 18:10;
>>> see also Ps. 5:11)

Others say that Christ prays for God to "keep them in [his] name" in terms of their loyalty to God. In other words, our Lord prays for us as God's children to be faithful to our Father's name; to always remember that we belong to and represent him. This seems to get to the sense of the prayer better, even though the former option remains true to Scripture and gives assurance of God's protection.

The name we are to be faithful to is the name given to Jesus by the Father. Since Jesus perfectly reveals the Father, as his true image bearer, he shares a name with the Father: "Therefore God has highly exalted him and bestowed on him the name that is above every name, so that at the name of Jesus every knee should bow, in heaven and on earth and under the earth, and every tongue confess that Jesus Christ is Lord, to the glory of God the Father" (Phil. 2:9–11). To be faithful to God, one must be faithful to his Son, and vice versa. As Jesus reveals the Father ("I have manifested your name"—John 17:6), we respond with faithfulness to God and Christ.

As D. A. Carson states:

> The name you gave me assumes that God has supremely revealed himself in Jesus. That is not only a dominant theme in

> this [John's] Gospel (1:18; 14:9), but entirely suits [chap. 17]
> vv. 6–8, "I have revealed your name to those whom you gave
> me out of the world." . . . In short, Jesus prays that God
> will keep his followers in firm fidelity to the revelation Jesus
> himself has mediated to them.[1]

What Christ requests here relates importantly to the saints' perseverance. This one request for loyalty to the "name" removes all uncertainties for the true child of God concerning perseverance. Jesus pleads with his Father to keep his disciples (and by extension, all disciples) faithful to the end. Are we to imagine that the Father will have Christ's request frustrated and unfulfilled?

John 17:11–12 speaks of God and Christ guarding and keeping the disciples. This reflects the heavenly pattern of Christ's priestly intercession. For example, in Hebrews 9:11–12 we read:

> But when Christ appeared as a high priest of the good things
> that have come, then through the greater and more perfect
> tent (not made with hands, that is, not of this creation) he
> entered once for all into the holy places, not by means of the
> blood of goats and calves but by means of his own blood,
> thus securing an eternal redemption.

The point is this: once saved by Christ (through his death), always saved by Christ (through his intercession). Jesus saves to the "uttermost those who draw near to God through him, since he always lives to make intercession for them" (Heb. 7:25).

Christ stresses the importance of our perseverance by grounding his appeal for it in the Father's name. In a sense, God's own reputation as the sovereign, gracious, unchanging, eternal Lord is at stake here. Will his power or sin determine the outcome?

Judas Was "Lost"

Christ's words about Judas in John 17:12 are indeed sobering. Rarely in the Bible do we hear of someone's eternal damnation. Jesus calls Judas the "son of destruction" (or "perdition"), which likely refers to his destiny but may also refer to his character. Earlier Jesus spoke of this harsh reality: "Jesus said to him, 'The one who has bathed does not need to wash, except for his feet, but is completely clean. And you are clean, but not every one of you.' For he knew who was to betray him; that was why he said, 'Not all of you are clean'" (John 13:10–11).

Judas was lost because the Father did not give him to Jesus. While an apparent follower of Christ who sat under his teaching, preached for him, and prayed with him, Judas in the end manifested his hypocrisy, wickedness, and hatred of the cause of Christ and his truth. Jesus speaks of this betrayal as the Scriptures being fulfilled. We learn the meaning of this from John 13:18, which quotes Psalm 41:9: "He who ate my bread has lifted his heel against me." This foreshadows Christ's betrayal.

Likewise, we find a pointer to the relationship between Jesus and Judas in the betrayed friendship between David and Ahithophel:

- Judas and Ahithophel both hang themselves after the deed (2 Sam 17.23/Matt 27.5).
- [Judas and Ahithophel] both plan to do the deed at night (2 Sam 17.1/John 13.30).
- David and Jesus both pray for deliverance on the Mount of Olives (2 Sam 15.31/Mark 14.26ff.).
- David and Jesus both cross the Kidron (2 Sam 15.23/ John 18.1).
- It is claimed that the death of one man will bring peace to the people (2 Sam 17.3/John 11.50).[2]

Ahithophel's betrayal of David exists as a type foreshadowing Judas's betrayal of Christ. These striking parallels clearly display God's sovereignty over these events (as over all), a sovereignty that never leaves the fulfillment of the Scriptures to chance. Jesus knew his "trusted friend" would betray him.

As Jesus prayed and confirmed before the Father various divine truths concerning his mission and our salvation, he was fully aware that fulfillment would come even through the deeds of wicked people. The path to Christ's glory necessarily and irreversibly led through the valley of shame. This included the wretched betrayal by one from his immediate group of twelve followers, the son of perdition.

We can only imagine how painful this prayer must have been for Jesus. Judas, made in God's image and given so many covenant blessings, ultimately rejected everything good for all that was bad. He got what he wanted in the end, tragically. Though he had received the very best teaching, discipleship, and pastoral care, he was filled with covetousness, hypocrisy, and treason—which led to suicide and, worse, eternal punishment.

Thus, when Christ prayed that the son of destruction (Judas) was lost, he acknowledged God's sovereign will in his own life. He knew he had been faithful in shepherding his disciples. He was not the immediate cause of Judas's betrayal; the Scriptures had to be fulfilled. The Father's plan had to unfold in a certain way.

15

Jesus Prayed for His Disciples to Be Joyful

John 17:13

But now I am coming to you, and these things I speak in the world, that they may have my joy fulfilled in themselves.

The Ground of Joy

Christ's disciples have no joy without his requesting it of the Father. In John 17:13 he asks that his disciples may know truths that sustain their mission on behalf of their Savior. What Jesus already prayed at the beginning of this prayer (John 17:1–5) would not really be clear until his post-resurrection instruction of his disciples (John 20).

The disciples could more fully understand and therefore enjoy true joy after Christ's triumphant resurrection and, later, his ascension to the Father. From there he currently protects the church by continually supplying her with grace from above. This he provides in his name by the power of the Spirit to the glory of God.

Earlier in John's Gospel our Lord spoke of his joy in relation to his disciples' joy: "As the Father has loved me, so have I loved you. Abide in my love. If you keep my commandments, you will abide in my love, just as I have kept my Father's commandments and abide in his love. These things I have spoken to you, that my joy may be in you, and that your joy may be full" (John 15:9–11). In these verses, Christ informs his disciples of the reality of their union with him. If they keep his commandments, he attests, they will abide in his love. This parallels the reality that he too remained in his Father's love by keeping his commandments. Keeping God's commandments connects explicitly not only to abiding in God and Christ but also to joy. In fact, Jesus spoke about "these things" in John 15 so that his disciples' joy "may be full" (v. 11).

If you take away Christ from this world—this incarnation as the God-man and his vicarious suffering for his people and resurrection from the dead—there exists no hope for God's eternal blessing and thus for true joy. Far from being joyful, we should weep constantly in the misery of this world, which provides nothing more than a temporary death chamber before we pass into nothingness. Yet Christ indeed rose from the dead, which means the hope of eternal joy remains for all who verbally confess and heartily believe that Jesus rose from the dead (Rom. 10:9).

Christ's Joy

Paul observed and so rejoiced in the Thessalonians: "And you became imitators of us and of the Lord, for you received the word in much affliction, with the joy of the Holy Spirit" (1 Thess. 1:6). Clearly affliction and Christian joy are meant to dwell together.

Christ, as God-man, experiences godly joy, a fruit of the Spirit (Gal. 5:22), because he possesses the Holy Spirit. We see Christ in the Old Testament as a "rejoicing" person. In Proverbs 8:30–31 the Son, as personified Wisdom, says,

> Then I was beside [Yahweh], like a master workman,
> and I was daily his delight,
>   rejoicing before him always,
> rejoicing in his inhabited world
>   and delighting in the children of man.

This verse describes Christ, the delight of the Father, rejoicing in God, the world, and the children of man.

While truly a "man of sorrows" (Isa. 53:3), Jesus was also a man of joy. He desired the same for his disciples. Remember, Jesus "rejoiced in the Holy Spirit" because the Father had revealed to "little children" the salvation that comes through his victorious conquest over Satan (Luke 10:21). He rejoiced that he defeated Satan, which produces in us godly confidence for both the present and the future. For all of the horrors of the cross, joy was set before him because he approached the cross by faith. He knew that God would make good on all his grand promises to the Son (Heb. 12:2).

Keeping God's commandments meant Jesus remained in his Father's love (John 15:10), and this brought our Savior great joy. The Father placed upon Jesus specific commandments, which included laying down his life for the sheep ("This charge I have received from my Father"—John 10:18). So, even in the trials of his self-giving sacrificial death, joy was never absent, because it was anchored in obedience to God.

Jesus is not speaking in John 17:13 of the infinite divine joy/blessedness that he possesses as the second person of the Trinity. We could not handle that joy, for it is ontologically impossible that we should share in that specific blessedness. It would destroy us, because it is a blessedness wrapped up in infinite, eternal, unchangeable power, glory, justice, and holiness. But, according to his humanity, in the power of the Spirit, Jesus knew and experienced a true spiritual joy that could be communicated to his disciples.

My Joy in Them

Jesus prays for disciples to receive his joy, but that occurs only through certain means God ordains. For example, Jesus tells his disciples: "Until now you have asked nothing in my name. Ask, and you will receive, that your joy may be full" (John 16:24). They need to ask. Jesus prays in John 17:13 what he already discussed with his disciples. Thus, these words should not surprise his disciples. What he previously taught them he now prays for them.

Paul asks the Philippians to rejoice: "Rejoice in the Lord always; again I will say, rejoice" (Phil. 4:4). As Thomas Watson rightly says, "Religion is no melancholy thing; it brings joy."[1] With the Lord at hand (Phil. 4:5), we need never be anxious but can pray assured of God's peace, which guards our hearts and minds in Christ (Phil. 4:6–7). Just as Jesus connected joy to union with him and keeping his commandments in John 15:9–11, Paul connects joy and peace with the following:

> Finally, brothers, whatever is true, whatever is honorable, whatever is just, whatever is pure, whatever is lovely, what-

ever is commendable, if there is any excellence, if there is anything worthy of praise, think about these things. What you have learned and received and heard and seen in me—practice these things, and the God of peace will be with you. (Phil. 4:8–9)

In other words, joy and peace bracket thinking about and living out what is good. We cannot have joy without peace, and vice versa.

Observe also that Jesus prays in such a manner that he wants us to share in all the good things he receives. He is not greedy, envious, or covetous. Rather, he is generous and kind and wants the best for us not just for himself, which would be the height of selfishness. As we consider what he knows and deserves, his desires to share his blessings with sinful humanity so clearly show why he is the Savior and Lord of God's people.

Following from this, we have a duty to pursue joy, which we will possess not as an optional but as a certain fruit of the Spirit (Gal. 5:22). Thomas Manton notes: "It is a sad thing that Christians should not have the wisdom to make use of their own felicity. . . . Oh! consider, sourness is a dishonor to God, a discredit to your profession, a disadvantage to yourselves, a grief to the Spirit, because you resist his work as a comforter."[2] If Jesus can be joyful going to the cross, should we not, who have the same Holy Spirit dwelling in us, be joyful in the midst of various trials?

We have every reason to be joyful. Christ in us, the hope of glory (Col. 1:27), is for us (Rom. 8:34) and wants us to be with him (John 17:24). We need to know who Christ is and what he prayed for, which allows us to ask (as we must) that his joy be fulfilled in us. For those who live by faith in the Son of God who loves us and gave himself for us (Gal. 2:20), this will certainly occur.

16

Jesus Prayed for His Disciples in the World

John 17:14–16

I have given them your word, and the world has hated them because they are not of the world, just as I am not of the world. I do not ask that you take them out of the world, but that you keep them from the evil one. They are not of the world, just as I am not of the world.

The Hatred of the World

The carnal mind is at enmity with God (Rom. 8:7) and his people (John 17:14). Jesus knew profoundly the hatred of the world when he prayed the words of John 17:14–16, with a view to soon leaving this earth and being seated in his glory at the right hand of God (Ps. 110:1). He also realized fully that, just as the world opposed him, it would show hostility to all who bear his name. Just as Christ spoke of joy to his disciples, in the upper room he also prepared them for the hatred they should expect from the world.

> If you were of the world, the world would love you as its own; but because you are not of the world, but I chose you out of the world, therefore the world hates you. Remember the word that I said to you: "A servant is not greater than his master." If they persecuted me, they will also persecute you. If they kept my word, they will also keep yours. (John 15:19–20)

The most basic reason why the world hates Christ and his disciples is that they are not of the world. The world hates foreigners who are utterly different from it. As John notes: "This is the judgment: the light has come into the world, and people loved the darkness rather than the light because their works were evil. For everyone who does wicked things hates the light and does not come to the light, lest his works should be exposed" (John 3:19–20). Or, similarly, "The world cannot hate you, but it hates me because I testify about it that its works are evil" (John 7:7).

Those given to Jesus from the Father receive an inestimable blessing that keeps them happy in God's presence for all eternity. Yet they were chosen out of the world to obey the words revealed to them from the Father through the Son. Because they are not of this world but are "of Christ" and obey his teachings, the world hates them.

Those not of the world are commanded frequently in the Scriptures to turn from the world and avoid loving it: "Do not love the world or the things in the world. If anyone loves the world, the love of the Father is not in him" (1 John 2:15). Christ knows that we have been given the capacity to love. But the question remains, what will we love? We will love either God or the world. We must not be conformed to the world if we want to live in communion with God and understand his will (Rom. 12:1–2).

Kept from the Evil One

The world, including nonbelievers and evil spirits doing Satan's work, is the realm alienated from God and in rebellion against him: "We know that we are from God, and the whole world lies in the power of the evil one" (1 John 5:19). Jesus gave himself to deliver us from the "present evil age" (Gal. 1:4). How should we respond?

Loving God and Christ remains the best corrective for loving the world. We do not simply hate the world because it presents nothing but an empty, hostile place that seeks to devour what is good, lovely, and pleasing in God's sight. We must have, as Christ's people, a love and affection that come from God and lead back to him, all in and through Christ and the Spirit. We are not of the world because we love God first and foremost, not ourselves or the world of which we are so much a part.

Without a doubt, Satan strives to devour God's people: "Be sober-minded; be watchful. Your adversary the devil prowls around like a roaring lion, seeking someone to devour" (1 Pet. 5:8; see also, Job 1:6–12; 2:1–6; 1 Cor. 5:5; 2 Cor. 2:11). Christ knew this well when he prayed the following for Peter: "Simon, Simon, behold, Satan demanded to have you, that he might sift you like wheat, but I have prayed for you that your faith may not fail. And when you have turned again, strengthen your brothers" (Luke 22:31–32).

The prayer here in John 17:15 for the disciples in general echoes the one offered up for Peter specifically. We have every assurance that such a request is offered for all believers, which makes our faithfulness possible. Jesus carries these requests into the heavenly places not only for Peter, James, John, and the disciples but also for all believers through the ages. We are kept from the Evil One by the Righteous One.

Not of This World

That Jesus is not of this world may be understood in light of his preexistence and incarnation as the God-man. His ontology (who he is; his being) makes "worldliness" impossible. He affirmed this in his dispute with the Jews in John 8. "He said to them, 'You are from below; I am from above. You are of this world; I am not of this world'" (v. 23).

The context in John 8 is not just ontological but also moral. Sent from heaven by his Father, Jesus is not from below. He stands against this world in its moral rebellion against God. The world hates Jesus due to his testimony against it (John 7:7). The world remains blind to truth and righteousness, which is why Jesus came teaching (John 6:45). The only escape for a world in sin is to believe in Jesus (John 8:24), the sinless Lamb of God who takes away the sins of the world (1 Pet. 1:19).

The moral excellence of Christ and the claims he made were reasons why he was hated. The more we are like him, the more we experience the same type of hatred.

Charles Spurgeon rightly emphasizes the need to be other-worldly in the way Christ was:

> This is the distinguishing mark—being different from the world in those respects in which Christ was different. Not making ourselves singular in unimportant points . . . but being different from the world in those respects in which the Son of God and the Son of man, Jesus Christ, our glorious example, was distinguished from the rest of mankind.[1]

Jesus did good (Acts 10:38) while testifying of its connection to the will of the Father. He did not glorify himself in such a life, since his "food" was to do the will of his Father (John 4:34).

When we live righteously for the sake of the kingdom and testify to the glory of Christ, we will inevitably face persecution. As Paul says in 2 Timothy 3:12, "Indeed, all who desire to live a godly life in Christ Jesus will be persecuted."

Likewise, Peter writes to the elect exiles of the Dispersion that no one can truly harm them if they show zeal for doing good (1 Pet. 3:13). Yet, as they imitate Christ and live in obedience to God, suffering matters not, since such godliness will lead to blessing from God (1 Pet. 3:14). They can have a good conscience, even amidst slander while, says Peter, "those who revile your good behavior in Christ may be put to shame" (1 Pet. 3:16). Being kept from the Evil One does not guarantee the absence of suffering. It does mean that we attain Christlikeness and so are kept from joining the world in its rebellion against God.

The world provides us with many snares and temptations. We do not stand a chance against the world without Christ praying the words of John 17:14–16. Prosperity, fame, power, and the temptations that come with them would chew us up and spit us out. Christ's words are not some magical formula but come from someone convinced of the efficacy of God's appointed means of prayer for keeping us from worldliness. Such faithfulness may bring with it poverty, shame, illness, and more. So Jesus's prayer is not about health, wealth, and fame, as the world understands these things.

The only prayers in Proverbs are instructive in relation to worldliness. Agur asks of God two things:

Two things I ask of you;
    deny them not to me before I die:

Remove far from me falsehood and lying;
> give me neither poverty nor riches;
> feed me with the food that is needful for me,
lest I be full and deny you
> and say, "Who is the LORD?"
or lest I be poor and steal
> and profane the name of my God. (Prov. 30:7–9)

Agur asks not only to be holy but also to be placed in an outward condition that avoids the temptations that come from poverty or riches. Wickedness and worldliness are no respecter of persons. As we pray that God would keep us from the temptations of the world and allegiance to the Evil One, we can be sure that we pray because Christ prays for us.

We need to be aware of who we are so that we can live in light of that reality. We are told that we are not of this world so that we will not live like it. Instead we are holy; therefore, we must live in holiness and fear of God.

17

Jesus Prayed for His Disciples to Be Sanctified

John 17:17–19

Sanctify them in the truth; your word is truth. As you sent me into the world, so I have sent them into the world. And for their sake I consecrate myself, that they also may be sanctified in truth.

Sanctification

No Christian would consider holiness a theological monster to be avoided at all costs. Yet holiness is not a terribly popular doctrine today, especially in North America and other parts of the (Western) world. Since Christ prays that his people will be sanctified, we must embrace the importance of holiness for the Christian faith (John 17:17).

One thing we all understand at a basic level is the fact that we are holy because God grants holiness to us. True enough! Yet the Scriptures make even more explicit claims about our holiness. The Father "consecrated" Christ when sending him into the world (John 10:36). God is "holy, holy, holy" (Isa. 6:3; Rev. 4:8). This means, of course, that Christ is holy, holy, holy (Isa. 6:1; John 12:41). But Christ receives consecration/sanctification as Mediator, which involves his full humanity. God sets his servants apart for religious purposes.

> Before I formed you in the womb I knew you,
> and before you were born I consecrated you;
> I appointed you a prophet to the nations. (Jer. 1:5)

God "sanctifies" his people with a view to preparing them for service. He then preserves them in this service of holiness (consecration). We should note that the Scriptures clearly emphasize this preservation (John 17:11, 16–17). God upheld no less than his servant Jesus.

> Behold my servant, whom I uphold,
>   my chosen, in whom my soul delights;
> I have put my Spirit upon him;
>   he will bring forth justice to the nations. (Isa. 42:1)

He upheld Jesus, but Jesus also actively consecrated himself as a sin offering for his people: "for their sake I consecrate myself" (John 17:19). We could not be holy or consecrated to God if Jesus did not first sanctify himself on our behalf (John 1:29). As one truly consecrated to God, Jesus did the will of the Father. He spoke his words, performed his works, and was totally and radically "set apart" to serve the true and living God. Filled with the Holy Spirit beyond measure (John

3:34), Jesus was and is God's supreme object of holiness in this world. We derive our holiness not immediately from God but through Jesus Christ, who prays for our sanctification through his own.

Thus, as J. I. Packer rightly notes concerning sanctification, it "is an ongoing transformation within a maintained consecration, and it engenders real righteousness within the frame of relational holiness." He says, "Relational sanctification, the state of being permanently set apart for God, flows from the cross, where God through Christ purchased and claimed us for himself (Acts 20:28; 26:18; Heb. 10:10)." In addition:

> Moral renovation, whereby we are increasingly changed from what we once were, flows from the agency of the indwelling Holy Spirit (Rom. 8:13; 12:1–2; 1 Cor. 6:11, 19–20; 2 Cor. 3:18; Eph. 4:22–24; 1 Thess. 5:23; 2 Thess. 2:13; Heb. 13:20–21). God calls his children to sanctity and graciously gives what he commands (1 Thess. 4:4; 5:23).[1]

Others have spoken of immediate sanctification and progressive, or definitive and progressive, or positional and progressive. Whatever the terminology, we are consecrated to God not as some future hope but as a present reality when we believe and we experience ongoing conformity to Christ's image.

There can be little doubt that Jesus intends both in his prayer that his people may be sanctified. He functions not as a partial or incomplete priest. He does not set us apart and then leave the rest to us. Rather, he sets us apart and continues the work in us that he began. He does this by his continued intercession through the means of his Word and Spirit.

By the Word

Jesus prays for his disciples to be like him: holy, sanctified, set apart, consecrated. But he does not pray for this to happen automatically. He prays explicitly that his disciples will be sanctified "in the truth" (John 17:17). Personally, I favor the rendering "by the truth." The means of sanctification are many (e.g., the Word, prayer, the sacraments). In this prayer, Christ asks God to sanctify his disciples by the truth, for Jesus is the truth (John 14:6). John Owen calls this part of the High Priestly Prayer the "blessed spring of our holiness."[2]

Jesus, as the one "in whom are hidden all the treasures of wisdom and knowledge" (Col. 2:3), desires that his disciples be sanctified not in the abstract through simply doing some undefined good and not evil. Instead, he seeks their sanctification by the truth that comes from God and through Christ. Christ is the content of the Word of God. It is nonsensical to say that Jesus, like Socrates, never wrote anything but was still a great teacher. Jesus, by the Spirit, penned the Scriptures so that they might reveal him.

As Christ made clear in the upper room, he would send the Paraclete to guide his disciples into all truth (John 16:13). What does this mean? Very simply, the Holy Spirit (the Paraclete) would glorify Christ. He proceeded from Christ to declare to the disciples the truth of Christ. Sanctification in the truth has the same goal as being conformed to Christ (Rom. 8:29). True holiness does not consist primarily in what we watch or do not watch, eat or do not eat, or drink or do not drink. Rather, it entails having the mind of Christ (1 Cor. 2:16) and living in this world while learning to think Christ's thoughts after him.

Naturally, the Word of God has many truths in the forms of promises, commands, warnings, and the like. They are all given, when rightly understood in the larger context of Christ and the gospel, to sanctify God's people.

The Word of God is not optional regarding our sanctification. As John Calvin vividly notes of this passage:

> [Christ] points out the means of sanctification, and not without reason; for there are fanatics who indulge in much useless prattle about sanctification, but who neglect the truth of God, by which he consecrates us to himself. Again, as there are others who chatter quite as foolishly about the truth and yet disregard the word, Christ expressly says that the truth, by which God sanctifies his sons, is not to be found anywhere else than in the word.[3]

For this reason, we must be continually reading and meditating on the Word and hearing it preached and taught, in order that we may learn of God concerning Christ. Our obedience, holiness, and likeness to Christ are related to the manner in which we approach and receive the Word. John Owen comments:

> How often in the reading of it do we meet with, and are as it were surprised with, *gracious words*, that enlighten, quicken, comfort, endear, and engage our souls! How often do we find sin wounded, grace encouraged, faith excited, love inflamed, and this in that endless variety of inward frames and outward occasions which we are liable unto![4]

God's Word, because it testifies to Christ, has a peculiar power whereby the Holy Spirit aims to glorify the Christ found in the Word, not a savior of our vain imaginations. In the words from Christ's mouth in John 17:17–19, we see why the Word and the Spirit should work true holiness in our souls. Owen rightly argues, "Nothing belongs to this holiness but what, in the actual communication of it, is a peculiar fruit of Christ's intercession."[5]

The Word wields power when the Spirit accompanies it. But the Spirit would not give power to the Word in our souls if Christ did not intercede for it. If God's Word comes to anyone with power, it does so because of the one "seated at the right hand of Power" (Mark 14:62).

As John Davenant (1572–1641) attested, "The love of God towards the regenerate is not founded in their perfection or absolute purity, but in Christ the mediator: as long as he intercedes their graces fail not."[6] We can be sure that the Word and Spirit will do their work because God loves us in Christ, who intercedes for us to be like himself. Thus, we can pray the words of Paul in 1 Thessalonians 5:23, "Now may the God of peace himself sanctify you completely, and may your whole spirit and soul and body be kept blameless at the coming of our Lord Jesus Christ."

18

Jesus Prayed for Church Unity

John 17:20–21

I do not ask for these only, but also for those who will believe in me through their word, that they may all be one, just as you, Father, are in me, and I in you, that they also may be in us, so that the world may believe that you have sent me.

Praying for His Bride

An important transition in Christ's prayer takes place in John 17:20–21, which extends beyond his immediate group of disciples to all believers of every age. We must take care not to over-emphasize the distinction between these two groups of followers, even though the latter believe through the preaching of the former. Jesus's petition here gives indication that "they" are not just the apostles but also the whole church through history. As Paul observes, we are all members of God's household, "built on the foundation of the apostles and prophets, Christ Jesus himself being the cornerstone, in whom the whole structure, being joined together, grows into a holy temple in the Lord" (Eph. 2:20–21).

The church enjoys a unique relationship with Jesus that the world does not. There never was or will be a saint in heaven not included in Christ's prayer of John 17:20–21. All who believe in him have faith because Christ's life, death, resurrection, and intercession make possible God's gracious gift of supernatural faith (John 1:12–13; 3:6–8; Eph. 2:4–10). The power to believe comes from Christ's intercession, whereby he sends the Spirit to bring light to those in darkness (Acts 2:33; Acts 26:18). Still, everyone coming to Christ must actively believe in him. He does not believe for us but prays for those who certainly will believe ("but also for those who will believe in me").

Belief through the Preached Word

Christ informs his disciples that they will bear witness about him. The Spirit, as the Spirit of Christ, bears witness about Christ (John 15:26; Rom. 8:9). The apostles will also bear witness about him because of their unique calling as those present with him from the beginning (John 15:27). Many interpreters focus so much on understanding the oneness expected for the church, they miss the point that faith comes through the preaching of the gospel. We must not miss this point. Hence, Jesus prays that the elect may come to faith through the apostles' "word," which refers simply to the Word of God in the name of Christ by the power of the Spirit.

Paul, as an apostle of Christ, makes this point clearly in Romans 10:14–15:

> How then will they call on him in whom they have not
> believed? And how are they to believe in him of whom they

have never heard? And how are they to hear without someone preaching? And how are they to preach unless they are
sent? As it is written, "How beautiful are the feet of those
who preach the good news!"

In his opening remarks in Titus, Paul likewise spells out plainly
the whole course of salvation in its basic parts:

Paul, a servant of God and an apostle of Jesus Christ, for the
sake of the faith of God's elect and their knowledge of the
truth, which accords with godliness, in hope of eternal life,
which God, who never lies, promised before the ages began
and at the proper time manifested in his word through the
preaching with which I have been entrusted by the command
of God our Savior. (Titus 1:1–3)

What Christ prays in John 17 concerns his servants' public
(and indiscriminate) preaching of the gospel for the salvation of
the elect. What Paul speaks of in Romans 10:14–15 and Titus
1:1–3 truly fulfills Christ's prayer.

God appointed the Word as the means to bring people to
faith in Christ because it testifies to him. God does not use means
unrelated to the ends. The "end" of our salvation is total conformity to Christ and communion with the triune God, which lead
to unending praise and adoration. If, for the sake of argument,
God used a "dream" to bring a Muslim to faith in Christ, that
dream would still necessarily be the word of Christ. Ordinarily
God uses the preached Word. When he uses some other means,
it can never be something divorced from content that speaks of
his beloved Son. Moreover, the Holy Spirit, in his work, glorifies
Christ. He performs not an act of magic but a work of Christ in
someone made alive in order to be remade, through the Word,
in the image of Christ.

Oneness

Jesus prays for those who will truly believe in him, through the means of the Word, that they will be united as "one." Paul greatly stresses such unity (the absence of division) in the church in many of his letters (see Eph. 3–4:16). The goal of the visible church is oneness (John 17:11, 21–23). Not surprisingly, given the history of the church, verses promoting oneness in John 17 have created significant debate (division?) among theologians from different backgrounds.

We should note that the oneness for which Jesus prays mirrors that between the Father and the Son:

- ". . . that they may be one, even as we are one" (John 17:11).
- "that they may all be one, just as you, Father, are in me, and I in you" (John 17:21).
- ". . . that they may be one even as we are one" (John 17:22).
- "I in them and you in me, that they may become perfectly one" (John 17:23).

Why highlight this? Because oneness in the Father and the Son and not unity in the church is the ultimate goal of Christ's High Priestly Prayer. Believers are "one" only in God and Christ.

Jesus knows deeply of his unity with the Father: "I and the Father are one" (John 10:30). Interestingly, John Calvin, comments on this:

The ancients made a wrong use of this passage to prove that Christ is (*homoousion*) of the same essence with the Father. For Christ does not argue about the unity of substance, but about the agreement which he has with the Father, so that whatever is done by Christ will be confirmed by the power of his Father.[1]

The English Puritan Thomas Goodwin takes a similar view: "The Father and the Son, though two persons, have but one will between them, and but one power between them. . . . John 10:30, 'My Father and I are one'; that is, have but one and the same power to save you, and one mind and will."[2] Of course, their unity of will and power in redemptive acts reflects an ontological unity between the two persons, which is why the Jews in John 10:31 pick up stones to stone Jesus.

At first glance, it seems most reasonable to argue that the oneness between the Father and Son concerns unity of essence. Yet believers cannot experience this with the divine essence, so this understanding must be dismissed. Instead, we ought to see the oneness between the Father and the Son as an expression of the unity of divine purposes and power in salvation. This qualification becomes necessary because Jesus wants unity in believers "as" such unity exists in the Godhead. In the accomplishment of God's work on earth, we must join with him in doing things the way he wants them done, not the way we think is best. Many churches, perhaps even unwittingly, are full of "earthly" purpose, not "heavenly" purpose.

Earlier, Jesus said: "The Son can do nothing of his own accord, but only what he sees the Father doing. For whatever the Father does, that the Son does likewise" (John 5:19). So, in John 10 Calvin and Goodwin see this in terms of the Father and Son carrying out salvation because of the immediate context.

> I am the good shepherd. I know my own and my own know me, just as the Father knows me and I know the Father; and I lay down my life for the sheep. And I have other sheep that

are not of this fold. I must bring them also, and they will listen to my voice. So there will be one flock, one shepherd. For this reason the Father loves me, because I lay down my life that I may take it up again. (John 10:14–17)

If the Father and the Son are one in purpose and love ("For this reason the Father loves me"—John 10:17), believers are to be likewise. The revelation of the Word of God concerning Christ, confirmed by his Spirit dwelling in us, is the means to bring that purpose to fruition. Our union with God and Christ by the Spirit gives us the power to be fruitful, as our Savior was for the kingdom (John 15:4–7).

Unfulfilled Prayer?

Has this prayer been answered for the church? Many bemoan its lack of fulfillment given the divisions within the church throughout history. We will come back to this concern, but first consider the probability that the desired fulfillment of such unity will occur only in the age to come. Still, it ought to have been the pursuit of the church since the time this prayer was first uttered. Not one believer escapes the implications of this prayer.

The church throughout history has experienced an abundance of schisms, as seen early on in the form of, for example, Montanism, Novatianism, and Donatism. Later, in 1054, came the East-West schism concerning, among other things, the filioque clause ("and from the Son") of the Nicene Creed, related to the procession of the Spirit. At the Colloquy of Marburg in 1529 the Lutherans and Zwinglians divided over the nature of Christ's presence in the Lord's Supper. Most Christians possess at least some awareness of the Roman Catholic–Protestant divide emerging during the sixteenth-century Reformation and the ongoing controversy over seeking to heal it. We could go on and on—sadly.

How are we to understand what Christ prays in light of what the church experiences? Understanding the nature of those for whom he desires oneness remains a good place to start. In our Lord's prayer for unity in John 17, he prays for those who know God (v. 3), are given to Christ by the Father (vv. 2, 6, 9, 24), have accepted God's Word (v. 7), are in the world but not of it (vv. 15–16), are sanctified by the truth (vv. 17–19), and are in union with Christ (vv. 21, 23, 26).

The visible church aims for peace and purity in her quest for unity. The unity for which Christ prays is not invisible but observable. The objects of his prayer can experience unity regardless of the denomination to which they belong. Yet their unity must exist in the truth. So unity cannot be experienced between true believers and those embracing a false gospel. Christ does not include in his prayer for unity any organized "Christian" denomination or quasi-Christian sect that rejects the gospel of free grace. Still, within those groups there may be individuals who believe the true gospel and embrace Christ as he is offered in it, in spite of what they are officially taught. Jesus certainly included such individuals in his prayer for unity.

The prayer of John 17:20–23 has been and is being answered, and one day will experience its ultimate fulfillment. The oneness Jesus seeks concerns not some future glory age experience by a remnant of the church. From the apostles to the last person converted before Christ returns, there exists oneness among Christ's true disciples. Jesus says, "There will be one flock, one shepherd" (John 10:16). Those within the flock are one with God, Christ, and each other. These people know the name of God (John 17:6) and all that means for them in their union with Christ.

Herman Ridderbos makes a crucial point that helps to relieve the ecumenical anxiety among those who read Christ's words and lament the apparent disunity in the church:

> It is evident from all this that the unity of the coming community is not considered here from the viewpoint of "being with each other" and still less from that of their calling and willingness to *form* a united group with each other and to organize and shape it in the most efficient manner. That, too, undoubtedly belongs directly or in a more derivative sense to Jesus' care for his church, even in his farewell discourse (cf. [John] 13:12ff.). But here the dominant thought of Jesus' prayer is that the church's unity may be controlled by, and find its criterion in, its unity with the Father and the Son, that is, in Jesus' coming into the world and his work in the world in keeping with *his* unity with the Father.[3]

Ridderbos strengthens his point by noting that the final words in 17:21 ("so that the world may believe that you have sent me") lead to the world believing Jesus was sent by the Father not because of perfect ecclesiastical unity but because of the "liberating power of Jesus' word and Spirit as it comes to expression in the church."[4] The church is made up of redeemed sinners who, despite their many failings and shortcomings—all of which will be finally dealt with by Christ as the Prophet, Priest, and King of the church—share a oneness with each other as beneficiaries of Christ's intercession that leads to life, glory, and vindication.

Pursuing truth, according to God's Word, in a manner consistent with the principles of pastoral care given to us in the Scriptures, is one way to be concerned for the unity Christ prays for. Oneness with God and Christ in establishing their purposes cannot happen apart from the true knowledge of God and Christ

(John 17:3)—which necessarily means that pursuing the truth is one way to pursue oneness. Hence the Reformers, for example, were correct to reject the teachings of Rome. Outwardly, some accused them of causing disunity, but the opposite was in fact the case. Truth, based on the gospel, was for the purpose of true oneness, not the bastardization of "oneness" offered by Rome.

19

Jesus Prayed for Us to Receive His Glory

John 17:22–23

The glory that you have given me I have given to them, that they may be one even as we are one, I in them and you in me, that they may become perfectly one, so that the world may know that you sent me and loved them even as you loved me.

Glory Given

The glory that Christ received as Mediator, which is not entirely the same as he possesses as the second person of the Trinity, can be "given" to the church. In this way, we may share in the oneness of purpose and privilege that exists between the Father and Christ. What an incredible blessing! We receive glory from God through Jesus Christ in the eternal life he provides. One day our glory will be to know the triune God by sight, without indwelling sin.

This glory comes not just in the future (in full) but immediately (in part). It occurs as we share in Christ's resurrection power and authority in our earthly Christian life through bringing the unsearchable riches of Christ to others. Broadcasting the good news, the gospel, becomes our glory. Because we are Christ's bride, his glory and our beauty go on display to the world. This can be appreciated only with the eyes of faith as we experience glory not simply as a future promise but also as a present reality. And this glory does not leave us stagnant but spurs us on to make known the glory of God and his Son. The Spirit, who loves this aim and purpose as the vicar of Christ, works within us to accomplish the purposes of the Father.

Mutual Indwelling

The Father and Christ the Mediator possess a unity of divine essence. But the Father communicates spiritual life (through the Holy Spirit) to Christ as God-man, according to his humanity. We see another sense in which the Father gives life to Christ in John 6:57: "As the living Father sent me, and I live because of the Father, so whoever feeds on me, he also will live because of me." The Holy Spirit is the means of communicating life from the Father to Christ and then from Christ to us. Earlier, Jesus similarly acknowledged, "For as the Father has life in himself, so he has granted the Son also to have life in himself. And he has given him authority to execute judgment, because he is the Son of Man" (John 5:26–27).

Isaiah prophesied of the Father's intention to pour out the Holy Spirit upon Christ, equipping him for his work as Mediator:

Behold my servant, whom I uphold,
  my chosen, in whom my soul delights;
I have put my Spirit upon him;
  he will bring forth justice to the nations. (Isa. 42:1)

How did people know that the Father was in Jesus? Our Lord answers that in John 10:37–38: "If I am not doing the works of my Father, then do not believe me; but if I do them, even though you do not believe me, believe the works, that you may know and understand that the Father is in me and I am in the Father." Christ, upheld by the Father, through the Spirit, did the works the Father gave him. There existed tangible, visible evidence that the Father was in Jesus because of what Jesus said and did. The Father mediated this power to Jesus through the Spirit of holiness.

Thus, if we are to share in this unity of purpose and mission in this world to the glory of God, the triune God must dwell within us (Eph. 3:17; Phil. 2:13). The Scriptures clearly show that all three persons of the blessed Trinity dwell in each believer in a special way that leads to love and communion between God and us.

Paul speaks of *Christ* in us in Romans 8:10: "But if Christ is in you, although the body is dead because of sin, the Spirit is life because of righteousness." This mirrors his language in Colossians 1:27: "To them God chose to make known how great among the Gentiles are the riches of the glory of this mystery, which is Christ in you, the hope of glory." Elsewhere, in rather glorious language, we are told that Christ dwells in our hearts "through faith" (Eph. 3:17).

Next, Paul considers the indwelling of the *Spirit* in Romans 8:11: "If the Spirit of him who raised Jesus from the dead dwells in you, he who raised Christ Jesus from the dead will also give

life to your mortal bodies through his Spirit who dwells in you."
The very Holy Spirit who raised Jesus Christ gives life to those
dead in their sin and takes up residence within us. This indwelling, which can never be lost, effects in us saving faith and a new
life united with Christ now and forever.

Finally, John speaks of the *Father* also dwelling in us in
1 John 4:12: "No one has ever seen God; if we love one another,
God abides in us and his love is perfected in us." The preceding
context of verse 9, which notes that "God sent his only Son,"
makes it clear that in verse 12 he considers God's abiding as
that of the Father. There you have it—something incredible and
yet seldom considered: the triune God in three persons, Father,
Son, and Holy Spirit, dwells within the heart of every believer!

This amazing truth about the indwelling triune God should
bring us great confidence. The Holy Spirit permanently abides in
us, though not because our holiness prompts him to do so. After
all, we are not holy in ourselves. Rather, the Spirit freely and graciously dwells in us with the Father and the Son, who are eternally
committed to each other. So, when they all take up residence in
God's people, we possess the certainty that if one abides, all three
do, since God is one. Likewise, we are assured that not one will
leave us, since that would mean departing from the other two.

Loved Like Christ

The last words of John 17:23 remain difficult for us to grasp, especially as we consider that the Father should love us "even as"
he has loved the Son. There is an infinite, eternal, omnipotent
love between the persons of the Trinity that suits them alone in
their divine essence. Ontologically, we cannot receive this type
of love because we cannot give it. Such mutual expressions are
limited to intra-Trinitarian divine love.

The Father loves the Son for his own sake. We are loved for Christ's sake. He is a natural Son; we are adopted children. The Father loves us because, through Christ, we are his children: "See what kind of love the Father has given to us, that we should be called children of God; and so we are. The reason why the world does not know us is that it did not know him" (1 John 3:1). If the Father loves Jesus as his beloved Son, we too will be beloved sons. The Father delights in Jesus not only because he is his Son but also because he acts like a faithful child toward his Father. The Father cannot help but offer public and private affirmations of his love for Jesus, in whom, as the highly favored one, he is well pleased (Isa. 42:1; Matt. 3:17; 17:5). Jesus always does what is pleasing to the Father (John 8:29).

As children of God, we receive an eternal love of benevolence from the Father that creates in us a disposition to love him in return. We cannot earn this love; it remains entirely unconditional. But in John 14:21–23 we are given a slightly different focus on God's love of complacency or delight in us as we respond to him with love:

> "Whoever has my commandments and keeps them, he it is who loves me. And he who loves me will be loved by my Father, and I will love him and manifest myself to him." Judas (not Iscariot) said to him, "Lord, how is it that you will manifest yourself to us, and not to the world?" Jesus answered him, "If anyone loves me, he will keep my word, and my Father will love him, and we will come to him and make our home with him."

Just as the Father loves the Son because of his faithfulness and obedience, so the Father will love us as we manifest the same. He will love us just as he loved Jesus. We need not worry whether this will happen. It occurs because Christ has prayed for it. The world must know of such delight the Father shows toward his obedient children.

God accepted Christ's obedience and rewarded it accordingly. In Christ and by the power of the Spirit, our imperfect faithfulness elicits God's reward as well. Outside of Christ, the Father can only reject our obedience. How can this be? Calvin provides the answer:

> Christ ever remains the Mediator to reconcile the Father to us; and his death has everlasting efficacy: namely, cleansing, satisfaction, atonement, and finally perfect obedience, with which all our iniquities are covered. And Paul does not say to the Ephesians that we have the beginning of salvation from grace but that we have been saved through grace, "not by works, lest any man should boast" [Eph. 2:8–9].[1]

With this reality of Christ's continuing work credited to us, Calvin attests that our works

> please [God] only when the person has previously found favor in his sight. And here we must faithfully keep the order to which Scripture leads us by the hand. Moses writes: "The Lord had regard for Abel and his works" [Gen. 4:4]. Do you see that he points out how the Lord is favorable to men before he has regard to their works? Therefore, purification of heart must precede, in order that those works which come forth from us may be favorably received by God."[2]

Since the Father delights in Christ's perfectly acceptable works, he likewise delights in our works in Christ. We are covered, which means our works are thereby covered by Christ's blood and made acceptable through the Spirit. God also rewards Christ for his works and will likewise reward his children for theirs. God does this in keeping with Christ's prayer, "You . . . loved them even as you loved me" (John 17:23).

In Christ's prayers we cannot help but be aware of his deeply personal relationship with the Father, which breathes out frequent affirmations of love. If there is one controlling aspect of true spiritual life that should accompany prayer, it is the reality that we are loved. For if God does not love us, then why even pray? But because God loves us in the same way that he loves his Son, how can we not pray?

20

Jesus Prayed for His People to Be with Him

John 17:24

Father, I desire that they also, whom you have given me, may be with me where I am, to see my glory that you have given me because you loved me before the foundation of the world.

Christ's Desire

What Jesus wants, he gets. For even the best saint, this degree of fulfillment would be disastrous, given our remaining sin. For unbelievers, it would bring utter devastation. But for the eternal Son of God who came to save sinners, the realization that he receives what he desires remains the incredible hope of the world.

In light of this, John 17:24 provides great comfort for those who lose a loved one in Christ. We all have to deal with such losses occasionally, and Christians even more, considering our extended family in the body of Christ. In the church we have—or at least we are supposed to have—many brothers, sisters, fathers, and mothers (Mark 3:31–35). And funerals become more frequent the older we get.

We all need to deal with the reality of death, not just our own but also with regard to those we know and love. Even though we triumph over it in Christ, death remains a real and frightening enemy: "The last enemy to be destroyed is death" (1 Cor. 15:26). Some of us have watched people die in front of us. Most of us have lost friends, young and old. Death is ugly and sorrowful. We rightly express our sorrow in the face of death even though Christians do not grieve as the world does (1 Thess. 4:13). Christ himself wept over the death of Lazarus (John 11:35). God has so designed us that death remains unnatural to us.

But when we lose a loved one in the Lord, John 17:24 helps us to deal with the sorrow that naturally overtakes us. This truth gets to the heart of the Christian religion and offers us insight into the person of Christ, the God-man. This verse gives us words that, on close and prayerful reflection, should be very near to our hearts when someone dies. Why? Consider the language: "Father, I desire that they also, whom you have given me, may be with me where I am, to see my glory that you have given me because you loved me before the foundation of the world."

As a man, Christ has had certain desires, first on earth and now in heaven. We may speak of "desiring God" and find that no one longed for him quite like Jesus did. But if you want to speak of "desiring man," you must also look to Christ, the God-man. He alone can yearn for both God and man in such a way that brings hope, reconciliation, and peace to God and humanity.

Christ makes his desire for his own known to the Father. He speaks, as he often did, of those given by the Father (see John 6:37, 39; 10:29; 17:6, 9). They are those for whom Christ laid down his life. The Good Shepherd lays down his life for the sheep (John 10:11), those he loves and naturally desires to be with him. In this way, even now, Christ holds certain unfulfilled longings in heaven, even though he remains there completely happy and satisfied.

How does this relate to the death of a loved one in Christ? Very simply, when a brother or sister in the Lord dies, Christ's prayer to the Father has been answered. So, when a Christian dies, the Father grants to his Son a request that began on earth.

In a believer's death, Christ gains a lot more than we lose. Likewise, the saints attain in heaven much more than they lost on earth. In the end, God, through his Son, and for his sake, never loses anything. When Christ gains, so do we. If God is for Christ and his bride, then gain is all there is for us.

True, we experience loss, sometimes beyond words, when a loved one dies. But the loss is never beyond Christ's words, "Father, I desire that they also, whom you have given me, may be with me where I am, to see my glory." Christ knows that his glory far exceeds the glories of anything this life can offer. The sight of him is worth more than millions of worlds and will leave no person unsatisfied. In this way, Christ exhibits a sense of "holy excitement" in seeking the eternal happiness of his people.

We certainly receive many joys on earth, but nothing compares with the joy of being in the heavenly presence of Christ. With a saint in his presence, Christ reaps the fruit of his work for sinners. This explains why we can weep buckets of tears and yet, in them, experience streams of joy running down our cheeks. Such losses present great tests of faith. Do we really believe that our beloved is better off with the Beloved than with us? If we do, then great joy accompanies terrible grief. Such joy comes as a precious gift from the One who grieved himself to neutralize our earthly grief. The death of a saint is "precious" in the eyes of the Lord (Ps. 116:15), in part because he takes him or her to himself. We too can know how precious this is, even in the greatest mourning.

To See My Glory

In this life we walk by faith, not by sight (2 Cor. 5:7). But faith in Christ, which transforms us into his image, will one day be changed into sight, and we shall be like him, for we shall see him (1 John 3:2). The principal object of our sight in glory shall be the image of the invisible God, Jesus Christ (Col. 1:15).

John Owen describes Christ's desire for us to see his glory:

> This alone, which is here prayed for, will give them such satisfaction, and nothing else. The hearts of believers are like the needle touched by the loadstone, which cannot rest until it comes to the point whereunto, by the secret virtue of it, it is directed. For being once touched by the love of Christ, receiving therein an impression of secret ineffable virtue, they will ever be in motion, and restless, until they come unto him, and *behold his glory*. That soul which can be satisfied without it,—that cannot be eternally satisfied with it,—is not partaker of the efficacy of his intercession.[1]

In other words, Christ's desire for us to see his glory becomes our own by the Spirit of Christ. In praying for us to see his glory, he imparts his own longing to us. For redeemed sinners, the exalted glory of Christ now remains, according to Owen, "too high, illustrious, and marvellous for us in our present condition. It hath a splendour and glory too great for our present spiritual visible faculty."[2]

In glory, we shall have an ocular vision of Christ: "They will see his face, and his name will be on their foreheads" (Rev. 22:4). As Thomas Manton says, "We need no other books than beholding his glory. . . . Christ in his glory and eminency is bible enough."[3] In beholding his glory we shall have a likeness and conformity to Christ, a love for Christ, and a delight in Christ.

Christ knows in his prayer of John 17:24 that the Father will reward him with the greatest possible glory a human can receive. We do not know the specifics of this glory, but Christ does and can only desire that we behold the love the Father poured out on him. In our seeing Christ's glory in heaven, the Father will be glorified. The Spirit shall enable us to apprehend Christ's glory—visible, intellectual, and spiritual—in a way that glorifies the three persons of the blessed Trinity. Owen rightly says:

> This makes me judge that the season of Christ's entrance into heaven, as the holy sanctuary of God, was the greatest instance of created glory that ever was or ever shall be, unto the consummation of all things. And this, as for other reasons, so because all the holy souls who had departed in the faith from the foundation of the world, were then received into the glorious light of the counsels of God, and knowledge of the effects of his grace by Jesus Christ.[4]

This "greatest instance of created glory" will become greater still when we "see the Son of Man coming in clouds with great power and glory" (Mark 13:26). Departed saints in this life are not at a loss compared with us. They will also not be at a loss when Christ returns (see 1 Thess. 4:13–17). They have the added advantage over living saints in the fact that they have seen Christ's glory already. Again, we mourn them, but we rejoice in the fulfilled desire of Christ to have them and theirs see his glory. Our loved ones in heaven—no better place to be.

21

Jesus Prayed with Confidence

John 17:25–26

O righteous Father, even though the world does not know you, I know you, and these know that you have sent me. I made known to them your name, and I will continue to make it known, that the love with which you have loved me may be in them, and I in them.

The Conclusion of the Matter

Jesus concludes his prayer with a tone of confidence before his righteous Father. He prays regarding himself and his great mission to make known the righteous saving actions of the God of Israel. In some ways, we might not want this ending to come yet. Admitted to the inner sanctuary of God, we hear these words between the eternal Son and Father of glory and are left wanting to hear and learn more. But even what we get is too much for us now.

The last express reference to the Father in this prayer as "righteous Father" indicates not only his character but also the nature of his activity to bring reconciliation through Christ between sinful man and a holy God (see Rom. 3:21–25). When the world fails to know God as the infinitely, eternally, unchangeably Righteous One, they know him not at all. Jesus knows and so loves God as righteous, and this gives Jesus confidence in his approach. Whatever happens to him comes from the hand of the One who is "righteous in all his ways" (Ps. 145:17).

Jesus (Alone) Knows God

Of all humankind born into this world after Adam's sin, only one can say he has truly known God. Jesus here would display stunning arrogance if this were not true. He claims not merely to know God but also to be the only person who does. Yet this is a privilege he does not keep to himself but shares with others so they can experience true knowledge of God. John's readers should not be surprised at Christ praying these words since the gospel provides other such testimony:

- "So Jesus proclaimed, as he taught in the temple, 'You know me, and you know where I come from. But I have not come of my own accord. He who sent me is true, and him you do not know'" (John 7:28).
- "They said to him therefore, 'Where is your Father?' Jesus answered, 'You know neither me nor my Father. If you knew me, you would know my Father also'" (John 8:19).
- "But you have not known him. I know him. If I were to say that I do not know him, I would be a liar like you, but I do know him and I keep his word" (John 8:55).

- "But all these things they will do to you on account of my name, because they do not know him who sent me" (John 15:21).

Yet, in all of this, Jesus equally emphasizes that he gives this knowledge to those given him by the Father: "I made known to them your name, and I will continue to make it known" (John 17:26). Jesus, by his Spirit, until he returns in glory, will make known the true and living God in a way that brings people to God (1 Pet. 3:18).

Jesus was brought to God himself by the Spirit. He knows the unspeakable joy of knowing and delighting in God. He loves every bit of knowledge from God and truly thirsts for him. We can marvel at Psalm 42:1–2, which provides words, in a sense, fully and properly true of Christ alone:

> As a deer pants for flowing streams,
>   so pants my soul for you, O God.
> My soul thirsts for God,
>   for the living God.
> When shall I come and appear before God?

Hence, Isaiah 50:4:

> The Lord GOD has given me
>   the tongue of those who are taught,
> that I may know how to sustain with a word
>   him who is weary.
> Morning by morning he awakens;
>   he awakens my ear
>   to hear as those who are taught.

When our Lord says, "I know you," he speaks of his human knowledge of the true God. His Father, through the Spirit, gave this knowledge to him from above. It was both natural and learned. By that I mean that he possesses all the treasures of wisdom and knowledge; but he also learned of and grew in them. If not, we struggle to make sense of the Bible, which frequently speaks of God's Messiah being taught by God:

- "So Jesus answered them, 'My teaching is not mine, but his who sent me'" (John 7:16).
- "I have much to say about you and much to judge, but he who sent me is true, and I declare to the world what I have heard from him" (John 8:26).
- "I speak of what I have seen with my Father, and you do what you have heard from your father" (John 8:38).
- "But now you seek to kill me, a man who has told you the truth that I heard from God" (John 8:40).

So, when our Lord prays the words "I know you," we need to realize that he affirms that he gleaned and responded to what God taught him. Christ's confidence in prayer is right and good, since he only speaks the truth. We, as Christ's people, who have been taught from him, need to and can get to the point where we too can say with confidence, "I know you" (see John 17:3).

Christ's Continued Work

Christ takes this prayer with him when he ascends into heaven and continually applies it to the spread of the gospel throughout the world. His words "and I will continue to make it known" find their explanation throughout John's Gospel, but especially early on: "The true light, which gives light to everyone, was coming into the world" (John 1:9). The light of the revelation of God through Jesus Christ continues to shine in this world because he has redeemed this world. Jesus as the Life continues to give life in this world (John 14:6).

What does it mean for Jesus to be the life and light of the world? The final words of John 17, "that the love with which you have loved me may be in them, and I in them," provide the answer. Jesus saves people from their sins in order that they may love God. Acceptable love toward God and Christ must come from God through Christ by the Spirit. We do not get love as a substance, as if it were the gift itself; we receive Christ himself. He dwells in us, along with the Father and the Spirit, so that we may receive what he requests in this High Priestly Prayer. Without a doubt, all is well for the Christian, based on this sole fact: "I in them." Christ in us is, as Paul said, the hope of glory (Col. 1:27).

If Christ is in me, I need fear nothing. He will be with me wherever I am. Whether I am in a house of mourning or of feasting, a hospital or sports stadium, ministering to the ungodly or praising God with the saints, he is with me. He has not left his people as orphans: "I will not leave you as orphans; I will come to you. Yet a little while and the world will see me no more, but you will see me. Because I live, you also will live. In that day you will know that I am in my Father, and you in me, and I in you" (John 14:18–20).

Jesus Prayed in Great Distress

Mark 14:32–34

And they went to a place called Gethsemane. And he said to his disciples, "Sit here while I pray." And he took with him Peter and James and John, and began to be greatly distressed and troubled. And he said to them, "My soul is very sorrowful, even to death. Remain here and watch."

Gethsemane

Nineteenth-century Scottish minister Hugh Martin skillfully guides his readers through the garden of Gethsemane and how Jesus faces there "the shadow of Calvary." The book by that very title remains, in my eyes, one of the finest treatments ever on the prayers of Jesus. Here Jesus's wrestling with submission to his Father's will causes our Savior more suffering and spiritual agony than even the physical brutalities of Golgotha could offer.

Gethsemane, meaning "olive press," was east of the Kidron brook, at the foot of the Mount of Olives. David and Jesus, in instances separated by close to a thousand years, suffered betrayal there by their trusted friends. They both had crossed the Kidron (2 Sam. 15:23; John 18:1) and prayed for deliverance near (or on) the Mount of Olives (2 Sam. 15:30–31; Mark 14:26–41). Praying in this location was evidently a custom of our Lord: "And he came out and went, as was his custom, to the Mount of Olives, and the disciples followed him" (Luke 22:39).

Most likely, Jesus prepared for this battle at Gethsemane in his previous prayer there. This would be the most ferocious battle of his life, because the realities of Golgotha were quickly being realized. The coming flood brought Jesus to a crisis point. Would he, the sinless one, be willingly swept away by the wrath of God or retreat to safety, leaving us as sinners to bear God's ferocious judgment?

We should not miss the biblical-theological significance of John walking us through the "garden" of Gethsemane (John 18:1). Remember reading in Genesis 2:8, "The LORD God planted a garden in Eden, in the east, and there he put the man whom he had formed"? Adam and Eve were tempted in that garden and failed miserably, bringing ruin and destruction upon the world. Jesus was tempted in a garden and triumphed gloriously on behalf of the elect. His response rectified Adam's act of rebellion that led to the death of all men, because all sinned in him.

Adam likely sinned in the daylight, bringing about spiritual darkness; Christ obeyed in the darkness, bringing about spiritual light. In fact, commenting on Gethsemane (Matt. 26:36–46), Matthew Henry writes: "The clouds had been gathering a good while, and looked black. . . . But now the storm began in good earnest."[1]

A. W. Pink highlights in more detail the contrasts between Eden and Gethsemane:

In Eden, all was delightful; in Gethsemane, all was terrible. In Eden, Adam and Eve parleyed with Satan; in Gethsemane, the last Adam sought the face of His Father. In Eden, Adam sinned; in Gethsemane, the Savior suffered. In Eden, Adam fell; in Gethsemane, the Redeemer conquered. The conflict in Eden took place by day; the conflict in Gethsemane was waged at night. In the one, Adam fell before Satan; in the other, the soldiers fell before Christ. In Eden the race was lost; in Gethsemane Christ announced, "Of them whom thou givest me have I lost none" (John 18:9). In Eden, Adam took the fruit from Eve's hand; in Gethsemane, Christ received the cup from His Father's hand. In Eden, Adam hid himself; in Gethsemane, Christ boldly showed Himself. In Eden, God sought Adam; in Gethsemane, the last Adam sought God! From Eden Adam was "driven;" from Gethsemane Christ was "led." In Eden the "sword" was drawn (Gen. 3:24); in Gethsemane the "sword" was sheathed (John 18:11).[2]

Greatly Distressed and Troubled

In the context of prayer, Jesus was "distressed and troubled." These words are uncommon in the New Testament. Word studies fail to give us complete understanding about what occurs here. Yet we get a glimpse into the intensity of his experience when Jesus testified, "My soul is very sorrowful, even to death" (Mark 14:34).

Remarkably, Jesus freely confessed his own struggles before men who had seen him "in power" (e.g., raising the dead, casting out demons). Peter, James, and John had witnessed the transfiguration (Matt. 17:1). Yet the Messiah's words must have stunned them, if indeed they had any idea what was really happening. Our Lord would never have overstated his trouble.

The sufferings of Job, the agony of Abraham leading his son Isaac to the altar, the grief of Joseph, David's sorrow over Absalom's death, and the many laments of the Psalms are pointers to the ultimate agony of Jesus, the only one undeserving of any despair in his life.

Only Jesus could understand what was awaiting him, because only he perfectly knew God. In turn, Christ's knowledge of God gave him confidence, joy, and a resolute spirit to do the Father's will. This knowledge triggered in him the affirmation of his soul's sorrow to the point of death. How could our Lord not have the piercing realities of Isaiah 53 racing through his mind at this point?

> Yet it was the will of the LORD to crush him;
>> he has put him to grief;
> when his soul makes an offering for guilt. (Isa. 53:10)

As already noted, Christ's life was a sort of perpetual Gethsemane, as Luke 12:50 seems to suggest: "I have a baptism to be baptized with, and how great is my distress until it is accomplished!" The flood of God's wrath would engulf the Savior.

> Your wrath lies heavy upon me,
>> and you overwhelm me with all your waves. (Ps. 88:7)

Additionally, Jonah's experience functioned as a type for the suffering endured by Christ.

> For you cast me into the deep,
>> into the heart of the seas,
>> and the flood surrounded me;

all your waves and your billows
    passed over me. (Jonah 2:3)

Jesus had only ever known the delight of the Father. He had pleasure in his God, who had the same in him, the highly favored one (Luke 2:40, 52). Yet Jesus here claimed a distress that was literally killing him. Hugh Martin well explains the reason for his troubled soul:

> Think of him consenting to have all the sins of myriads imputed to him by his Father: to underlie, that is, the imputation, in his Father's judgment, of every kind and degree and amount of moral evil—every species and circumstance and combination of vile iniquity! There is a book of reckoning which eternal justice writes in heaven, where is entered every charge to which infinite unsparing rectitude, searching with omniscient glance alike the darkness and the light, sees the sons of men become obnoxious.[3]

To be a merciful High Priest, able to sympathize with all who belong to him as a faithful Shepherd, Jesus had to experience such despair. In this way, no one can ever say, "Nobody knows the trouble I've seen." Jesus had to suffer in this way—to the point of death—because he must identify (and beyond) with the pain of his people. Jesus must be not only the eminently righteous but also the suffering one. Consider how the experience described in various psalms of lamentation looked ahead to Christ in Gethsemane:

> With my voice I cry out to the LORD;
>   with my voice I plead for mercy to the LORD.
> I pour out my complaint before him;
>   I tell my trouble before him.

When my spirit faints within me,
  you know my way!
In the path where I walk
  they have hidden a trap for me.
Look to the right and see:
  there is none who takes notice of me;
no refuge remains to me;
  no one cares for my soul. (Ps. 142:1–4)

Christ endured such sorrow because he knew such solitude in his moment of crisis: "Remain here and watch" (Mark 14:34). He had to be alone, for the battle he waged against principalities and powers remained his alone. But that did not make it easy for him in his isolation of sorrow:

Joy is a partnership,
Grief weeps alone;
Many guests had Cana,
Gethsemane but one.

                    F. L. Knowles (1869–1905),
                        Grief and Joy

23

Jesus Prayed for Deliverance

Mark 14:35–36

And going a little farther, he fell on the ground and prayed that, if it were possible, the hour might pass from him. And he said, "Abba, Father, all things are possible for you. Remove this cup from me. Yet not what I will, but what you will."

Falling Down

Mark informs us that Jesus "fell on the ground." Matthew adds, "And going a little farther he fell on his face and prayed" (Matt. 26:39). With Christ's soul at the point of death, we should not expect him to march triumphantly around praising God. Many times people stand in prayer. For example, Hannah did so after the birth of Samuel: "Oh, my lord! As you live, my lord, I am the woman who was standing here in your presence, praying to the LORD" (1 Sam. 1:26). God's people also spread

179

out and lift up their hands and also bow their heads (Neh. 8:6). At other times they will lift up their eyes to heaven: "I lift up my eyes to the hills" (Ps. 121:1). Daniel knelt toward Jerusalem (Dan. 6:10). As Christ did here, many also fell down prostrate, such as Abraham, Moses, and Aaron (Gen. 17:3; Num. 14:5). Ezra and the Israelites did the same: "And Ezra blessed the LORD, the great God, and all the people answered, 'Amen, Amen,' lifting up their hands. And they bowed their heads and worshiped the LORD with their faces to the ground" (Neh. 8:6).

Our Lord would have prayed in all of these various positions, as was fitting the occasion. But here, in physical and emotional distress, he must have fallen. Soon, others fell while seeking Jesus when he announced, "I am he," at which point "they drew back and fell to the ground" (John 18:6). The one with power to make Roman soldiers and Jewish officers fall with his words, he was the one falling before his God prior to their coming for him.

Christ's Request

Only Mark records Jesus calling God "Abba." The other Gospels manifest the Greek address (*patēr*), meaning "Father." "Abba" transliterates the original Aramaic Jesus would have used as an address of intimacy. Without a doubt, Jesus addressed the Father here deeply conscious of a unique relationship with him. No one but the eternal Son of the Father could enter and fully appreciate and understand such a relationship.

The God-man, as sinless, righteous, undefiled, must always submit in his human will to the will of the Father. But in Jesus's true humanity, the battle he faced was by no means easy. This point requires careful consideration, and may God give us all grace to say neither too much nor too little about this event in his life.

The words of Christ in Gethsemane are clear as he asked the Father to remove the cup (of wrath) from him. Jesus desired to avoid this trial. I agree with Hugh Martin, in his wonderful book *The Shadow of Calvary*, that if Jesus had not petitioned the Father for the cup to pass, we might rightly call into question his sinlessness. If he had not begged the Father three times, "Remove this cup," we could rightly question whether he possessed any real human sense of the holiness of God. No one understood this like the Son of God, who would soon experience the full fury of God's holiness. And if he did not shrink back from that, we might question this man's sanity and even wonder if he went to his death as a masochist. In other words, to be sinless (as he was) and to confront a holy God at Golgotha but be counted a sinner in God's presence there—this explains why Christ would not naturally want to be in such a position.

Appropriately and without sin, he petitioned, "Remove this cup." From all eternity and from the time he was born, he had only ever known the smile and favor of the Father and the loving communion they shared. Now, with the prospect of his Father turning away from him, how could he not ask, "Remove this cup from me"?

Martin wonderfully explains this petition:

Considered simply in itself, to desire exemption from the wrath of God was the dictate of his holy human nature, considered at once sensitive and reasonable and holy. Not to have felt this desire, instead of being holiness unto the Lord, would have argued—what we tremble even to think of while we know it could not be—daring contempt of the divine anger and will! Nay: to have such impressive views as Jesus now had of his Father's wrath, and not be filled with an earnest longing to escape from it . . . would have argued that he did not possess a true human nature with all the sinless sensibilities which are of the essence of humanity.[1]

Nevertheless, all of Christ's requests for the cup to be removed were wrapped in the words "Your will be done," which fulfill the words of Isaiah 50:5,

> I was not rebellious;
> I turned not backward.

The Father's Response

Jesus knew that his Father possessed the power to release him from the "cup" of impending horrors awaiting him: "All things are possible for you" (Mark 14:36). This reality only makes the agony of Christ's prayer more intense. Note well: we must never think that God here displayed impotence, the inability to help.

God possesses an absolute power denoting not what he will necessarily do but what he could possibly do. Likewise, he displays an ordained power, indicating what he has chosen to do in his eternal purpose to foreordain all things (Eph. 1:11). Jesus himself knows the difference, saying at his arrest moments later: "Do you think that I cannot appeal to my Father, and he will at once send me more than twelve legions of angels? But how then should the Scriptures be fulfilled, that it must be so?" (Matt. 26:53–54).

God could have, according to his absolute power, sent more than twelve legions of angels to rescue Christ from his passion, but, according to his ordained power, he did not. This helps us to understand the Father's response to Jesus. Remember, when Satan tempted Jesus to turn stones into bread to prove he was God's Son, Jesus trusted God instead and appealed to the Scriptures, which were his rule of life (Matt. 4:3–4). So here the Father's "answer," had he given one, could have been, "Yes,

I can remove this cup from you; but what does my Word say concerning your life?"

Going back a little earlier, we can be reasonably certain that Jesus had the Word of God and all it testified concerning him firmly before him. For example, when he went with his disciples to the Mount of Olives, he said to them, "You will all fall away, for it is written, 'I will strike the shepherd, and the sheep will be scattered.' But after I am raised up, I will go before you to Galilee" (Mark 14:27–28). Jesus knew what the Old Testament Scriptures testified, as he quoted Zechariah 13:7 ("Strike the shepherd, and the sheep will be scattered") to his disciples. He thus received his answer from God in the way we are to receive answers from the Lord: "Well, the Word of God says . . ." After all, when the angel of the Lord told Abraham not to lay a hand on Isaac, that angel (Jesus) knew that he would be the "ram" to sacrificially take Isaac's place on the altar. It is everywhere written in the Old Testament concerning what Jesus came to do, and explicitly affirmed by Christ throughout his own ministry.

Christ's Response

From the beginning of his public ministry Jesus affirmed over and over that he came to die for sinners:

- "For even the Son of Man came not to be served but to serve, and to give his life as a ransom for many" (Mark 10:45).
- ". . . just as the Father knows me and I know the Father; and I lay down my life for the sheep" (John 10:15).

Fully aware of his mission, Jesus also knew that he must and would do the will of the Father. As the author of Hebrews notes, when Jesus came into the world he said:

Sacrifices and offerings you have not desired,
  but a body have you prepared for me;
in burnt offerings and sin offerings
  you have taken no pleasure.
Then I said, "Behold, I have come to do your will,
    O God,
    as it is written of me in the scroll of the book."
    (10:5–7)

Jesus's prayer necessarily led him to decisively choose, as God's servant, to do his Father's will instead of serve himself. He thus served God and his children, not shrinking back, but fully resolved to obey even to the point of death on a cross (Phil. 2:8). Jesus likely prayed the petitions of Matthew 6:10 frequently during his life:

Your kingdom come,
your will be done,
    on earth as it is in heaven.

His resolve for this was severely tested in the garden.

The End of the Matter

Scottish theologian Thomas Crawford (1812–1875) made this fitting observation about Gethsemane: "There is something deeply mysterious in this passage of our Lord's history. It seems scarcely a fit or a becoming thing to pry into it. Nor can we speak of it without feeling that we speak inadequately, and fearing that we may speak amiss."[2]

What can we say about the fact that the God-man, full of grace and truth and beloved of the Father, prayed to the point of needing angelic assistance (Luke 22:43)? How can we understand Jesus praying "in agony" and praying "more earnestly" so that "his sweat became like great drops of blood falling down to the ground" (Luke 22:44)? It is beyond us to understand.

Jesus, in obedience to the will of God, went out from the garden, at this point, treated like a criminal in every way. Fallen Adam had words of grace spoken in regard to him after his departure from the garden (Gen. 3:15). In contrast, Christ was taken from the garden, bearing the wrath of God and the hatred of man because of his righteousness.

The German Reformed preacher F. W. Krummacher (1796–1868) makes these profound comments regarding this scene in Christ's life:

> The voice which resounded through the Garden of Eden cried, "Adam, where are you?" But Adam hid himself trembling, behind the trees of the garden. The same voice, and with a similar intention, is heard in the Garden of Gethsemane. The second Adam, however, does not withdraw from it, but proceeds to meet the High and Lofty One, who summons him before him, resolutely exclaiming, "Here am I!"[3]

Here am I. I have come to do your will. Even if it must take me to the most abhorrent place possible, nevertheless your will be done. If it means my shrieks, as from one in hell itself, nevertheless your will be done. If it means crying out, "My God, My God, why have you forsaken me?" nevertheless your will be done. Here am I. I have come to do your will.

24

Jesus Prayed for His Enemies

Luke 23:34

And Jesus said, "Father, forgive them,
for they know not what they do."

Living What He Preached

Our Lord preached many sermons during the course of his ministry (Mark 1:38), one of the most famous of which instructed his followers to love their enemies and pray for their persecutors (Matt. 5:44). True sons of the Father act like him (Matt. 5:45). Jesus knew, of course, that one day this command would test him to the fullest. Could he pray for those crucifying him? Would he, by praying for his enemies, prove himself to be the true Son of his heavenly Father?

In the context of Luke 23, Christ's enemies are Jews and Romans, both of whom were responsible for his death. When they did their very worst against him, he gave his very best for them. In his agony and distress, he did not become self-focused. He turned to prayer. Naturally, he called upon his Father, this time not to remove his bitter "cup" of wrath but to forgive the sins of those who heinously acted against him, the Lord of glory (1 Cor. 2:8).

Jesus found himself in a position where all he could do was pray for others. He prayed not for mere onlookers but for those showing tangible hatred. This was a perfect occasion for Christ to live out his own preaching ministry. And he did so in the most spectacular way possible: "Father, forgive them, for they know not what they do" (Luke 23:34).

Prophecy Fulfilled

In this short prayer, filled with grace and mercy toward those who deserved wrath and justice, we have the fulfillment of Christ's mission as the promised Old Testament Messiah.

> Therefore I will divide him a portion with the many,
>   and he shall divide the spoil with the strong,
> because he poured out his soul to death
>   and was numbered with the transgressors;
> yet he bore the sin of many,
>   and makes intercession for the transgressors.
>   (Isa. 53:12)

There was really no other alternative for Christ in this moment. Just as Isaiah prophesied, the Messiah would pour out his soul to death as a sin-bearing sacrifice. Yet the prophet also claimed that God's servant would make intercession for the transgressors. Might this particular text have flashed through Christ's mind when he prayed for the forgiveness of his enemies?

Whatever the case, Jesus publicly fulfilled the prophecy regarding his role as not only a sacrifice but also an Intercessor.

Sinful Ignorance

In this brief prayer to the Father, our Lord claims that his enemies are ignorant of what they do. This claim seems odd at first glance. Christ's enemies knew, of course, that they were crucifying him, and many even cried out these very words, "Crucify him" (Luke 23:21).

In Acts 3:17, Peter preaches to his listeners, informing them that they "acted in ignorance, as did also [their] rulers." Acts 13:27 provides a clue to Christ's claim, when Paul observes of Christ's haters, "For those who live in Jerusalem and their rulers, because they did not recognize him nor understand the utterances of the prophets, which are read every Sabbath, fulfilled them by condemning him." Elsewhere Paul says that the rulers of this age were ignorant of God's purposes in Christ; otherwise, "they would not have crucified the Lord of glory" (1 Cor. 2:8).

Put simply, those who killed Jesus failed to know him not only as the Messiah but also the divine Son of God. As Jesus attested, "They know not what they do." Yet we must also recognize that these adversaries also displayed ignorance of Yahweh. They did not understand God's purposes in Christ. They thought, many of them, that they were on the Lord's side doing him a favor by killing a blasphemer: "And the high priest tore his garments and said, 'What further witnesses do we need? You have heard his blasphemy. What is your decision?' And they all condemned him as deserving death" (Mark 14:63–64).

The Jewish religious leaders, along with the Romans, Pilate, Herod, and others, failed to recognize that God was in Christ and for Christ. They knew not that they were resisting God by opposing Christ. So, when Jesus turned to the Father in prayer, he showed awareness of himself as God's faithful representative, instead of the Jews who thought they were faithful by executing him. Even with their ignorance, they remained guilty. Consequently, Christ prayed for their forgiveness.

Forgiveness Available to All

If anyone should be excluded from the offer of forgiveness, it should be those heinously responsible for the shameful murder of the Lord of glory. Against such we could certainly understand Jesus bearing a grudge. Yet Jesus embraces them in love.

Jesus shows true love to the worst of sinners. Love is "patient and kind. . . . Love bears all things . . . endures all things" (1 Cor. 13:4, 7). Is there a greater display of love and forgiveness in action than Christ praying on the cross for those who put him there? Can anyone accuse Christ of not practicing what he preached? Can anyone say he did not love his enemies? His attitude of mercy toward his oppressors provides a mighty example for his followers.

This is not pie in the sky theology, reserved for Christ alone to practice. Peter tells his readers that in his suffering, our Lord left us an example, "so that you might follow in his steps" (1 Pet. 2:21). Stephen, during his own horrific execution, both exemplified the response of Christ and provided a pattern for other Christians: "And as they were stoning Stephen, he called out, 'Lord Jesus, receive my spirit.' And falling to his knees he cried out with a loud voice, 'Lord, do not hold this sin against them.' And when he had said this, he fell asleep" (Acts 7:59–60).

In praying the way he did on the cross, Jesus not only blessed his enemies; he also benefits us, making it possible for us to pray the same way in the face of persecution. Prayer for those who oppress us remains one of the most soul-enriching things we can do. We all want assurance as sons of our heavenly Father, and we gain such assurance by lifting up in prayer those who hate us.

25

Jesus Prayed with a Loud Cry

Mark 15:34

And at the ninth hour Jesus cried with a loud voice, "Eloi, Eloi, lema sabachthani?" which means, "My God, my God, why have you forsaken me?"

A Cry

Jesus wanted to be heard. This was true from the beginning until the very end of his earthly ministry. Jesus also wants to be heard in heaven, which his words of intercession in John 17 show.

Yet, during and despite his physical sufferings, including a crown of thorns placed on his head and nails driven through his flesh, and despite his emotional anguish, including that inflicted by a jeering crowd, Jesus remained silent. Such silence manifested his faith in his Father and added weight to the silence-breaking cry of dereliction "Eloi, Eloi, lema sabachthani."

These Aramaic words, quoting Psalm 22, are haunting. The experience of being forsaken remains one of the most terrifying realities for human beings, indeed, even animals. When a child loses Mom or Dad, a cry quickly emerges as a natural human response to a terrifying situation. At Calvary, our Lord prayed to God in a manner that we can never fully appreciate. Indeed, only Christ has understood the words he cried out to God, words that must have stunned even the angels in heaven.

This cry took place after three hours of darkness. Darkness can be symbolic of God's judgment, such as in Egypt when the plague of darkness covered the land for three days (Ex. 10:21–23; see also Joel 3:15; Amos 8:9; Rev. 6:12; 8:12). The darkness in Mark's description of the crucifixion clearly signifies God's judgment on sin. Jesus, as the Sin-Bearer, bore that very judgment.

The words Jesus cried out remind us of the shrieks of those who are cast away forever. These words from Psalm 22:1 were, in a sense, foreign to Christ to this point. Jesus had been the constant delight of the Father, who publically displayed his love for his Son: "Behold, a voice from heaven said, 'This is my beloved Son, with whom I am well pleased'" (Matt. 3:17). But then Christ descended into a type of hell where he was forced to cry out in agony.

In hell a pain of sense and a pain of loss are both experienced. Christ's human nature suffered both the pain of sense (physical and emotional torments) and the pain of loss (the withdrawal of his Father). The Puritan John Flavel (1627–1691) remarks, "So upon Christ answerably, there was not only an impression of wrath, but also a subtraction or withdrawing of all sensible favor and love."[1]

The only appropriate response from Christ while he experienced the bitter desertion of all sensible favor from his Father was to cry out. This cry came not from a madman who made no sense. Rather, even in his distress, the words of God were on his lips. He continued relating to his Father in an appropriate manner regardless of his misery.

We have much to learn from this in our own heavenward cries, which must always be lawful and never self-indulgent. We must care for God's wisdom and not merely our release from affliction.

Losing the Love of the Father?

Does Christ's cry of dereliction mean he lost the infinite love of the Father? The answer must be an unequivocal no, for many reasons.

To suggest Jesus lost the infinite love of the Father is to say several things far from the truth:

- There was a time when Trinitarian love was not.
- There was a time when the person of the Father did not love the person of the Son. That is to say, "God did not love God."
- God did not love Christ's consummate act of obedience on the cross.
- God was not pleased with such obedience to his own will.
- The words of Christ in John 8:29, "I always do the things that are pleasing to him," are false.
- God, who loves all creatures, loved a frog more than his Son at the time of crucifixion.

To say that Jesus lost the love of the Father will not do. After all, argues Calvin: "How could he be angry toward his beloved Son, 'in whom his heart reposed' [cf. Matt. 3:17]? How could

Christ by his intercession appease the Father toward others, if he were himself hateful to God?"[2]

Herman Witsius (1636–1708) makes the point that when Christ voluntarily went to the cross as our substitute, the love of the Father was not in any way diminished. "On the contrary, he never pleased the Father more, than when he showed himself obedient unto death, even the death of the cross. For this is that excellent, that incomparable, and almost incredible obedience, which the Father recompensed with a suitable reward of ineffable glory."[3]

Given the doctrine of divine simplicity, to say that Jesus lost the infinite love of the Father seems to imply a breakdown in the divine nature itself. This remains an unthinkable conclusion that entirely undermines the original premise of absolute divine power and love in salvation. It also plays into the hands of contemporary critics of penal substitution, as it presents such a gross disunity within the Godhead.

For these reasons, we must tread very carefully. If Jesus did not lose the love of the Father, then how can we explain the words of dereliction?

Forsakenness

Jesus never wavered in his faith or faithfulness, even on the cross. He entrusted himself to God his Father. His perfect theology demanded that he knew, better than we ever can know, that his Father's love for him could never be extinguished or even diminished.

Even as God's children, we can feel abandonment acutely while just as keenly aware of his abiding and continual love. Our cries are real and significant. How much more the cry of the eternal Son.

The Father made Christ so sensible of his place as a con-demned criminal that his cry of dereliction arose out of his Fa-ther's "frowning providence." In this way, the Father allowed his Son to truly feel the horrors all around him, essentially grant-ing him a glimpse into hell itself as he hung from the cross. The darkness, the jeering, the sight of his mother and loved ones, the delight of his fellow Jews at his death, the venom of the Roman soldiers, the abandonment of his disciples, and the betrayal by Judas—together they launched a deluge upon his soul. At this time, Jesus experienced, in his humanity, total isolation and abandonment. At the same time, he possessed full awareness that God was publicly placing a curse upon him; he cut Jesus off from the land of the living (Isa. 53:8).

Jesus knew his Father's favor, but according to his humanity he intensely experienced horror, loneliness, grief, and forsaken-ness. He needed an outlet for his emotional state. Psalm 22:1 provided the perfect expression of such. He boldly bewailed his abandonment.

Incidentally, this perhaps explains how Christ could be "made perfect" as a High Priest (Heb. 5:9). Until this point, he had not known the hiddenness of God. But then he experienced Psalm 88, specifically the hidden "face" of God (v. 14), allowing him to minister to those who endure the terrors set forth in the psalm. To be a merciful High Priest to those who feel utterly for-saken by God, Christ had to undergo the cross and the desertion connected with it. Only then was he equipped to sympathize with us in every way. In other words, becoming a merciful High Priest demanded that Jesus enter heaven through Golgotha.

Reading the words "My God, my God," we can be sure that Jesus did not waver in his faith. True, he did not say, "Fa-ther," but in the context of quoting Psalm 22, he was not merely "proof-texting" on the cross. That is to say, the use of Psalm 22:1 should not be isolated from the rest of the psalm and the psalmist's faith. For example:

> But you, O LORD, do not be far off!
>> O you my help, come quickly to my aid!
> Deliver my soul from the sword,
>> my precious life from the power of the dog!
>>> (Ps. 22:19–20)

Our Lord did not receive an immediate rescue, but his God was not far off. He would vindicate his Son and raise him from the dead. Thus, when Jesus howled out the words of forsakenness, they remained full of faith and confidently looked to God to uphold him and care for him despite the horrors he felt at the time.

26

Jesus Prayed His Final Prayer

Luke 23:46

Then Jesus, calling out with a loud voice, said, "Father, into your hands I commit my spirit!" And having said this he breathed his last.

Final Words

One's dying words can be a testimony to how he or she has lived. We cannot predict with certainty what we will say at such a time, but we do know the last words of the Lord. They comprised, fittingly, a public prayer before many witnesses. Jesus could have prayed quietly or even silently, but instead he made sure that his final words were heard.

Those present who condemned him as a blasphemer did not ultimately cause Jesus any doubt about his own identity. Far from it. They only strengthened his assurance as God's faithful

Messiah. The servant remained faithful to the end. All Old Testament prophecy concerning the Messiah's sufferings (Psalm 22; Isaiah 53) had been fulfilled.

We are not sure how many times during his earthly life Jesus uttered the title "Father." Certainly, he used the name consistently and on a daily basis, especially as cultivated by an intense prayer life: "In the days of his flesh, Jesus offered up prayers and supplications, with loud cries and tears, to him who was able to save him from death, and he was heard because of his reverence" (Heb. 5:7). In his prayer of Luke 23:46, all that remained was the Father's reception of his Son's spirit. This petition would be surely answered, as evidenced by Jesus's promise to the repentant dying thief that they would be in paradise "today" (Luke 23:43).

What Is Not Assumed Is Not Healed

The incarnation of the Son of God was the enfleshment of the eternal Son. This means that Jesus became fully man with a true body-soul composite. In this way, he is not a soul with a body, nor a body with a soul.

On the cross, the Son of God died. Jesus as a person died. That is why we can say, "God died on the cross" (see Acts 20:28); natures do not do things in the abstract. However, we must avoid—even by implication—the grotesque, heretical, and blasphemous idea that God, in his simple divine essence, can die. The God-man, Jesus Christ, died on the cross. While he died as a person, he did so according to his human nature. When Jesus offered himself up on the cross by the eternal Spirit (Heb. 9:14), his body was eventually committed to the grave, but his soul to his Father. There was a temporary separation of body and soul, just as there is for God's people who die in this world as their soul goes to be with the Lord, but their body goes to the grave.

The majority of Reformed theologians in the post-Reformation era adopted the view that to say Christ "descended into hell"—a phrase from the Apostles' Creed also rendered "descended to the dead"—was another way of stating that he was buried in the earth. As the Westminster Larger Catechism states, "Christ's humiliation after his death consisted in his being buried, and continuing in the state of the dead, and under the power of death till the third day; which hath been otherwise expressed in these words, he descended into hell" (Q. 50). This connects "descended into hell" not with his burial in the earth but with his enduring the state/power of death; that is, "which" modifies not "buried" but "continuing." This makes sense with the language of the creed "was crucified, died, and was buried [thus WLC 50, "buried"]; he descended [thus WLC 50, "continuing"] to the dead."

Jesus knew his body was going to be preserved from decay in the grave (Acts 13:35). But he also knew that his soul/spirit would be immediately in the presence of his Father upon death. Christ had great faith that he would not be condemned, despite taking our place as a condemned person. His confidence in God was both *public* and *vicarious*.

Christians can have the same type of confidence as Christ at death, because of how he approached it. He took away our sins, so that we can call on God as Father. He lived the life of which we are incapable, so that we can pray each day, like the psalmist,

Into your hand I commit my spirit;
    you have redeemed me, O Lord, faithful God. (Ps. 31:5)

Christ has redeemed us, both soul and body. Jesus assumed a true body-soul in order to rescue ours. Jesus may have quoted this part of Psalm 31 at other times before this. Interestingly, he added the word "Father," removed the words "you have redeemed me," and retained the words "into your hands I commit my spirit." This seems quite appropriate in light of everything we have learned about Christ's person and prayer life. The eternal Son of the Father came to redeem as a true man who, in death, needed to commit his soul to his Father.

Answered Prayer

Jesus lived a life whereby he could say each day, "Into your hands I commit my spirit." He did not do his own thing, expecting one day to simply cast himself on God in the vain hope he would be in a "better place," as many non-Christians suggest. He lived in constant communion with his Father so that when his final hour came, he would do what was normal to him on a regular basis. His quote of Psalm 31:5 was a natural expression for him. Obviously he could have used other words, but the basic prayer would have been the same.

He was about to die, and his hope to be with the Father was about to be realized. Until Christ's soul could be reunited with his body at the resurrection on the third day, his soul was in the presence of God. This was a unique redemptive-historical experience for Jesus. His incarnation happened in history with a created body-soul that subsisted in the person of the Son. But when his soul went to heaven and his body went to the grave, Jesus was truly in the grave and in heaven at the same time; the union between his body and his soul was not ultimately severed, but since one was immaterial and one was material, they were in distinct places.

When believers die, our glory remains while our bodies and souls are in distinct places. We long for the reunion of our bodies and souls, knowing that at the resurrection it will occur. They can never be ultimately severed from one another. But they are separate from one another for a time at death. Why? Because we are united to Christ in body *and* soul, not just one *or* the other.

Jesus possessed a union with God in his person that could never be severed. His soul went immediately to paradise, not to hell, as some vainly imagine. He had lived by faith all his earthly life. But at his death he would enter the realm of sight. He would see the place prepared not just for God's people but also for him to reign as King (Ps. 110:1). In all of the terrors he endured on the cross, the light emerged from darkness. He would soon be in a place of power and prestige with a name that is above every name (Phil. 2:9).

We can be sure that when Christ finally breathed his last, these words were uttered in heaven, then later again at the triumphant ascension of Christ with his risen and glorified body:

> Lift up your heads, O gates!
> > And be lifted up, O ancient doors,
> > that the King of glory may come in.
> Who is this King of glory?
> > The LORD, strong and mighty,
> > the LORD, mighty in battle!
> Lift up your heads, O gates!
> > And lift them up, O ancient doors,
> > that the King of glory may come in.
> Who is this King of glory?
> > The LORD of hosts,
> > he is the King of glory! Selah. (Ps. 24:7–10)

The King of glory prayed on his way to glory, where he ever lives to pray for the saints. We can be so thankful for the prayer life of Jesus. There is no hope without it, but every hope because of it.

Notes

Introducing Our Praying Lord

1. John Anthony McGuckin, *Saint Cyril of Alexandria and the Christo-logical Controversy* (Crestwood, NY: St. Vladimir's Seminary Press, 2004), 133.

2. As Francis Turretin remarks, "It is one thing to speak of the whole Christ; another to speak of the whole of Christ. The whole Christ is God and man, but not the whole of Christ. Whole in the masculine (*totus*) denotes a person in the concrete, but whole in the neuter (*totum*) a nature in the abstract. Therefore it is rightly said that the whole Christ is God or man because this marks the person; but not the whole of Christ because this marks each nature which is in him." *Institutes of Elenctic Theology*, trans. George Musgrave Giger, ed. James T. Dennison Jr., vol. 1 (Phillipsburg, NJ: P&R, 1992), 13.7.17.

3. Hugh Martin, *The Shadow of Calvary* (London: Counted Faithful, 2017), 36.

Chapter 1: Jesus Prayed from His Mother's Breasts

1. While I speak of Christ's "religious life" for his life of faith whereby he sang, read God's Word, prayed, attended festivals, went to the temple, cared for the needy, and so forth, I am also aware that we must not make Jesus the first "Christian." We stand in a religious relation to Jesus since he is the object of our faith. J. Gresham Machen's *Christianity and Liberalism* is a powerful corrective to the theological liberalism that made Jesus simply a believer in God like us. While we can speak of a "religious life" in reference to the Son of God, we must not forget that he is the object of our worship because he is the God-man.

2. Charles Spurgeon, *The Treasury of David*, vol. 1 (Nashville: Thomas Nelson, 1984), 327.

3. John Calvin, *Institutes of the Christian Religion*, ed. John T. McNeill, trans. Ford Lewis Battles (Philadelphia: Westminster Press, 1960), 4.16.18.

4. David M. M'Intyre, *The Hidden Life of Prayer and the Prayer-Life of Our Lord* (Hannibal, MO: Granted Ministries, 2012), 88.

Chapter 2: Jesus Prayed "Abba! Father"

1. Joachim Jeremias, *The Prayers of Jesus* (Philadelphia: Fortress, 1989), 57.

2. Charles Spurgeon, *Spurgeon's Sermons on Prayer* (Peabody, MA: Hendrickson, 2007), 358.

Chapter 4: Jesus Prayed the Lord's Prayer

1. See Gordon J. Bahr, "The Use of the Lord's Prayer in the Primitive Church," *Journal of Biblical Literature* 84, no. 2 (June 1965): 153–57.

2. John R. W. Stott, *The Message of Ephesians* (Downers Grove, IL: InterVarsity Press, 1979), 157.

Chapter 6: Jesus Prayed Knowing He Would Be Heard

1. Sinclair Ferguson, *In Christ Alone: Living the Gospel-Centered Life* (Lake Mary, FL: Reformation Trust, 2007), 147.

Chapter 7: Jesus Prayed for His Father's Glory

1. St. John Chrysostom, "Homilies on the Gospel of Saint John," in *Nicene and Post-Nicene Fathers*, series 1, ed. Philip Schaff, vol. 14 (Peabody, MA: Hendrickson, 1999), 249.

Chapter 8: Jesus Prayed for His Own Glory

1. Thomas Manton, *The Complete Works of Thomas Manton*, 22 vols. (Worthington, PA: Maranatha, 1970), 10:122.

Chapter 9: Jesus Prayed concerning Eternal Life

1. John Calvin, *Calvin's Commentaries*, vol. 18, *John 12–21, Acts 1–15*, trans. William Pringle (repr., Grand Rapids, MI: Baker, 1996), 73 (on John 13:31).

Chapter 10: Jesus Prayed for Us to Know God and Himself

1. John Calvin, *Calvin's Commentaries*, vol. 18, *John 12–21, Acts 1–15*, trans. William Pringle (repr., Grand Rapids, MI: Baker, 1996), 166–67 (on John 17:3).

2. John Owen, *The Works of John Owen*, ed. William H. Goold, 16 vols. (1850–1855; repr., London: Banner of Truth, 1965–1968), 2:35–36.

Chapter 11: Jesus Prayed for the Glory He
Had Before the World Existed

1. Thomas Goodwin, *The Works of Thomas Goodwin*, 12 vols. (repr., Grand Rapids, MI: Reformation Heritage, 2006), 4:485–86.
2. Goodwin, *Works*, 4:486.
3. John Owen, *The Works of John Owen*, ed. William H. Goold, 16 vols. (1850–1855; repr., London: Banner of Truth, 1965–1968), 1:55.

Chapter 12: Jesus Prayed concerning God's Self-Disclosure

1. Stephen Charnock, *The Works of Stephen Charnock*, vol. 4, *A Discourse of the Knowledge of God in Christ* (Edinburgh: Banner of Truth, 2010), 4:131.
2. Charnock, *Works*, 4:132.
3. Charnock, *Works*, 4:135.

Chapter 13: Jesus Prayed for the Elect to Glorify Him

1. Thomas Manton, *The Complete Works of Thomas Manton*, 22 vols. (Worthington, PA: Maranatha, 1970), 10:242.
2. D. A Carson, *The Gospel according to John*, The Pillar New Testament Commentary (Grand Rapids, MI: Eerdmans, 1991), 560.
3. Stephen Charnock, *Discourses on Christ Crucified* (London: Religious Tract Society, 1830), 83.
4. John Owen, *The Works of John Owen*, ed. William H. Goold, 16 vols. (1850–1855; repr., London: Banner of Truth, 1965–1968), 10:91.
5. Owen, *Works*, 10:90.
6. Manton, *Works*, 10:246.
7. Thomas Watson, *A Body of Divinity* (1692; repr., Edinburgh: Banner of Truth, 2000), 181.
8. Manton, *Works*, 10:260.
9. Manton, *Works*, 10:261.

Chapter 14: Jesus Prayed That the Father Would Protect the Church

1. D. A. Carson, *The Gospel according to John*, The Pillar New Testament Commentary (Grand Rapids, MI: Eerdmans, 1991), 562.
2. M. J. J. Menken, *Old Testament Quotations in the Fourth Gospel: Studies in Textual Form* (Kampen: Kok, 1996), cited by Steve Moyise, *The Old Testament in the New: An Introduction*, 2nd ed. (London: T&T Clark, 2015), chap. 4, e-book.

Chapter 15: Jesus Prayed for His Disciples to Be Joyful

1. Thomas Watson, *A Body of Divinity* (1692; repr., Edinburgh: Banner of Truth, 2000), 272.

2. Thomas Manton, *The Complete Works of Thomas Manton*, 22 vols. (Worthington, PA: Maranatha, 1970), 10:359.

Chapter 16: Jesus Prayed for His Disciples in the World

1. Charles Spurgeon, *Spurgeon's Sermons on Prayer* (Peabody, MA: Hendrickson, 2007), 431.

Chapter 17: Jesus Prayed for His Disciples to Be Sanctified

1. J. I. Packer, *Concise Theology: A Guide to Historic Christian Beliefs* (Wheaton, IL: Tyndale, 1993), 169.

2. John Owen, *The Works of John Owen*, ed. William H. Goold, 16 vols. (1850–1855; repr., London: Banner of Truth, 1965–1968), 3:506.

3. John Calvin, *Calvin's Commentaries*, vol. 18, *John 12–21, Acts 1–15*, trans. William Pringle (repr., Grand Rapids, MI: Baker, 1996), 179–80 (on John 17:17).

4. Owen, *Works*, 4:192–93.

5. Owen, *Works*, 3:506.

6. John Davenant, cited in *View of Some Divine Truths*, by Edward Polhill (London: A.M. and R.R. for T. Cockerill, 1678), 75.

Chapter 18: Jesus Prayed for Church Unity

1. John Calvin, *Calvin's Commentaries*, vol. 17, *Harmony of Matthew, Mark, Luke, and John 1–11*, trans. William Pringle (repr., Grand Rapids, MI: Baker, 1996), 417 (on John 10:30).

2. Thomas Goodwin, *The Works of Thomas Goodwin*, 12 vols. (repr., Grand Rapids, MI: Reformation Heritage, 2006), 4:81.

3. Herman Ridderbos, *The Gospel of John: A Theological Commentary* (Grand Rapids, MI: Eerdmans, 1997), 561.

4. Ridderbos, *John*, 561.

Chapter 19: Jesus Prayed for Us to Receive His Glory

1. John Calvin, *Institutes of the Christian Religion*, ed. John T. McNeill, trans. Ford Lewis Battles (Philadelphia: Westminster Press, 1960), 3.14.11.

2. Calvin, *Institutes*, 3.14.8.

Chapter 20: Jesus Prayed for His People to Be with Him

1. John Owen, *The Works of John Owen*, ed. William H. Goold, 16 vols. (1850–1855; repr., London: Banner of Truth, 1965–1968), 1:286.

2. Owen, *Works*, 1:290.

3. Thomas Manton, *The Complete Works of Thomas Manton*, 22 vols. (Worthington, PA: Maranatha, 1970), 11:104.

4. Owen, *Works*, 1:264.

Chapter 22: Jesus Prayed in Great Distress

1. Matthew Henry, *An Exposition of the Old and New Testaments*, 3 vols. (London: Robinson, 1828), 3:227.
2. Arthur W. Pink, *Exposition of the Gospel of John*, vol. 3 (Grand Rapids, MI: Zondervan, 1956), 157–58.
3. Hugh Martin, *The Shadow of Calvary* (London: Counted Faithful, 2017), 31.

Chapter 23: Jesus Prayed for Deliverance

1. Hugh Martin, *The Shadow of Calvary* (London: Counted Faithful, 2017), 19.
2. Thomas Crawford, *The Doctrine of Holy Scripture Respecting the Atonement* (London: William Blackwood, 1871), 127.
3. F. W. Krummacher, *The Suffering Saviour* (repr., Edinburgh: Banner of Truth, 2004), 100.

Chapter 25: Jesus Prayed with a Loud Cry

1. John Flavel, *The Works of John* , vol. 4 (repr., Edinburgh: Banner of Truth, 2015), 352–53.
2. John Calvin, *Institutes of the Christian Religion*, ed. John T. McNeill, trans. Ford Lewis Battles (Philadelphia: Westminster Press, 1960), 2.16.11.
3. Herman Witsius, *Conciliatory, or Irenical Animadversions on the Controversies Agitated in Britain, Under the Unhappy Names of Antinomians and Neonomians*, trans. Thomas Bell (Glasgow: W. Lang, 1807), 44.

General Index

abba/Abba, 38, 40, 42, 180
Adam and Eve
  disobedience of, 100
  temptation of, 174
adoption, 41, 157
Agur, 135–36
Ahithophel, 123–24
Alexandrian theologians, 17, 20
already–not yet, 64
"And Can It Be?" (hymn), 22
angels, 56, 109
anhypostatic human nature, 20
Antiochene school, 17
Apostles' Creed, 201
appropriations, 94
Arianism, 71, 104
assurance, 121
Augustine, 104

beholding Christ's glory, 164–65
believing in Christ, 144
Bellarmine, Robert, 21
body and soul, 200, 202

Calvin, John, 31, 86–87, 92, 141,
  146–47, 158, 195–96
Cameron, John, 113
Carson, D. A., 114, 121–22
Chalcedonian Creed, 16, 74
Charnock, Stephen, 108–9, 115

"chief end" of man, 73–74, 77
children, prayer habits of, 34–35
children of God, 40, 41, 157
Christlikeness, 135
Christology, 15
Chrysostom, 76
church, 143–44
  heavenly purpose of, 147
  schisms in, 148–49
  unity of, 146–51
circumcision, 28
communication of properties, 18,
  21–22
communion with God, 44, 47, 133
communion with the Father, 95, 97
communion with the Son, 97
confidence, 201
consecration, 138
corporate solidarity, 28, 58
corporate worship, 49
Council of Chalcedon, 16
Crawford, Thomas, 184
cross
  and attributes of God, 86
  glorifies the Father, 85
  glory of, 82
cup of God's wrath, 56, 59,
  181–82, 188
Cyril of Alexandria, 15, 17, 20, 23

211

daily bread, 56–57
Daniel, prayer of, 44, 58, 89, 180
darkness, 194
Davenant, John, 142
David and Ahithophel, 123–24
death, of loved one in Christ, 162–66
definitive sanctification, 139
Didache, 52
divine simplicity, 196
Donatism, 148

"earthly" purpose, 147
East-West schism, 148
Eden, 175
Edwards, Jonathan, on private prayer, 48–49
elect, prayer of Jesus for, 113–18
Elijah, 69
enhypostatic human nature, 20
enmity with God, 131
eternal glory, 83–84
eternal life, 88–90, 97
Eutyches, 17
experience, as great teacher for prayers, 29

faith
  becomes sight, 164
  comes through preaching of the gospel, 144–45
false gospel, 149
Father
  authority of, 87
  delights in our works in Christ, 158
  dwelling in us, 156
  first in order of subsistence, 94
  gives all things to the Son, 114
  heard prayers of Jesus, 70–71
  love for the Son, 156–57
  paternity of, 40
  reception of the Son's spirit, 200
  sends the Son, 94
"Father in Heaven," 52–53
fear of God, 136
Ferguson, Sinclair, 69
"finite not capable of the infinite," 19
Flavel, John, 194
forgiveness, 57–58, 190
forsakenness of Christ, 196–98
"frowning providence," 197
fruit of the Spirit, 62, 127
funerals, 162

Gethsemane, 56, 74, 75–77, 173–78, 181–85
glorifying Christ, 116–18
glorifying God, 73–74, 77–78
glory, through suffering, 83
glory of God, 77
God
  ad extra works of, 94
  attributes of, 86
  covenant faithfulness of, 28
  hiddenness of, 197
  holiness of, 181
  immanence of, 53
  listens to obedient worshipers, 68–70
  love of benevolence, 157
  love of complacency, 157
  personal properties of, 22
  as Righteous One, 168
  self-disclosure of, 107–10
  sovereign will of, 66
  transcendence of, 53
godliness, 69, 116
godly fear, 71
Golgotha, 181
Goodwin, Thomas, 103–4, 147

habit of faith, 29
habits of grace, 32
hallowing the name of God,
    53–54, 78
Hannah, 179
heavenly glorification, 117
hell, 194
Henry, Matthew, 174–75
High Priestly Prayer, 53, 72, 83,
    140, 146
holiness, 136, 137–42
    and prayer, 69
Holy Spirit
    as bond of love in Trinity, 39
    declares the truth of Christ, 140
    indwelling of, 155–56
    and joy, 62–63
    and joy of Christ, 127
    in the life of Christ, 22–25
    poured out upon Christ, 154–55
    as Spirit of adoption, 39–41
hypostatic union, 18, 19, 23

ignorance, of Christ's enemies, 189
imitation of Christ, 135
incarnation, 126
intercession, 115. *See also* Jesus
    Christ, intercession of

Jeremias, Joachim, 38
Jesus Christ
    addressed God as "Father,"
        37–39
    anointed with the Spirit, 62
    ascension of, 120, 126, 203
    authority of, 87–88
    baptism of, 25, 58
    birth of, 82
    communion with the Father, 202
    confidence in prayer, 110
    cry of dereliction, 193–98
    death as baptism, 77

death of, 115, 200
descended into hell, 201
desires of, 162–63
distressed and troubled in Geth-
    semane, 175–77
divine nature of, 18–19, 23–24,
    102
exaltation of, 84
faithful covenant child, 27–28,
    30
faithful servant to the end, 200
filled with the Spirit, 138
forsakenness of, 196–98
glory as God-man, 117
glory as Mediator, 153–54
glory in heaven, 165
heard by the Father, 70–71
human nature of, 18–19, 20, 24,
    26, 102, 194
humiliation of, 18, 103, 105,
    201
intercession of, 111, 115–18,
    119–22, 139, 188, 203
joy of, 61–66, 126–28
knows the Father, 168–70
as life and light of the world,
    170–71
life of as perpetual Gethsemane,
    54, 74, 75, 80, 176
"made perfect" as High Priest,
    197
as Mediator, 21, 93, 102, 108,
    111, 114
mediatorial authority of, 88
natural glory of, 117
as new "Daniel," 43–44
obedience of, 77–78, 84,
    100–101, 183
prayed for his own glory,
    99–105
prayed in agony, 184–85

prayed in secret, 43–49
prayed the Psalms, 33, 34, 58
prayer for deliverance, 179–85
prayer for disciples in the world, 131–36
prayer for enemies, 114, 187–91
prayer for the elect, 113–18
presence in the Lord's Supper, 148
priesthood of, 115
as Prophet, Priest, and King, 56, 58, 120
religious life of, 30, 205n1 (chap. 1)
as representative person, 58
resurrection of, 70, 125, 202
as sacrifice, 115, 188
as second Adam, 185
as servant/Messiah, 111
soul of, 24, 74–75, 77
temptation in Gethsemane, 59, 174
temptation in the wilderness, 82, 182
two natures united in single person, 16–17, 20
unity with the Father, 146–47, 203
in us, 155
wept over death of Lazarus, 162
wrestling in prayer, 56, 59, 173
Jonah, 176–77
joy, 61–66, 125–29
as fruit of the Spirit, 62, 127
and peace, 128–29
and truth, 64–65
and will of God, 65–66
Judas, betrayal of, 123–24

kingdom of God, coming of, 54–55, 64
knowing Christ, 89, 92–93, 96–97

knowing God, 91–97
Knowles, F. L., 178
Krummacher, F. W., 185

Lamb's Book of Life, 65
Lazarus
death of, 162
raising of, 70–72
"light for the nations," 101
Logos, 20
Lord's Prayer, 51–60, 64
first petition, 53–54
second petition, 54–55
third petition, 55–56
fourth petition, 56–57
fifth petition, 57–58
sixth petition, 58–59
Lord's Supper, 57, 148
love
for enemies, 187, 190
for God, 132–33
for the world, 132–33
loyalty to God, 121–22
Lutherans
Christology of, 18–19
on the Holy Spirit, 23

Machen, J. Gresham, 205n1 (chap. 1)
"man of sorrows," 127
Manton, Thomas, 83, 113–14, 115, 118, 129, 165
Marburg Colloquy, 148
Martin, Hugh, 25–26, 173, 177, 181–82
Mary, 17, 27
McGuckin, John Anthony, 15
Messiah, suffering of, 200
M'Intyre, David M., 32
Montanism, 148
morning prayers, 44
Mount of Olives, 174, 183

name of God, 53–54, 78, 121
    manifested by Christ, 109–10
name of Jesus, 121
Nestorianism, 17, 22
Nestorius, 15
new life, 116
Nicene Creed, 148
Novatianism, 148

obedience, 111–12, 135, 158
oblation, 115
Old Testament Scriptures, 120
oneness of the church, 146–51
Owen, John, 23, 95, 104–5, 114,
    115, 140, 141–42, 164–65

Packer, J. I., 139
peace, and joy, 128–29
persecution, 135, 191
perseverance, 122
Peter, Christ's prayer for, 133
Pink, A. W., 175
prayer
    as gift, 69
    as intimate conversation with
        the Father, 39
    and love of God, 159
    as preparation, 47–48
    as private devotion, 43–49
present evil age, 133
private worship, 49
progressive sanctification, 139
Proverbs, prayers in, 135–36
Psalms, 33, 34, 58
public worship, 47, 49
Puritans, 22

quiet time, 49

reconciliation, 94–95
redemption, of body and soul,
    200–201

Reformed Christology, 19, 20–22
rejoicing, 63
resurrection, 202
Revelation, as glorification of the
    Son, 84
reward, and private prayer, 48
Ridderbos, Herman, 150
"righteous Father," 168
Roman Catholic Church
    Christology of, 18–19, 21
    false unity of, 151
    on the Holy Spirit, 23

sanctification, 137–42
Satan
    defeat of, 54, 64
    temptation of Jesus, 182
    work of, 133
sin
    hinders prayer, 67
    ignorance of, 189–90
Son. *See also* Jesus Christ
    assumed human nature, 74, 102
    faithfulness and obedience of,
        157–58
    glorification of, 79–84
    life of Trinitarian activity, 34
    reconciles us to the Father,
        94–95
    prayer life of, 34, 37
sonship, 41
Spurgeon, Charles, 30–31, 41, 134
Stephen, 190
Stott, John, 55
strength in weakness, 46

temptation, 58–59, 82, 135
thanksgiving, 56–57, 62–63
theological liberalism, 205n1
    (chap. 1)
theotokos, 17
trials, 45

Trinity, 74
  dwelling in each believer,
    155–56
  economic language, 94
truth
  and sanctification, 140
  and unity, 150–51
Turretin, Francis, 205n2 (intro.)

union with Christ, 41–42, 126,
    148, 203
union with God, 148
Upper Room Discourse, 80

"watch and pray," 59
Watson, Thomas, 116, 128
Western church, Christology of, 18
Westminster Confession of Faith, 21

Westminster Larger Catechism,
  201
Westminster Shorter Catechism,
  16, 73, 77–78
will of God, 55–56, 65–66, 76–77,
  81
Witsius, Herman, 196
Word, as means of bringing people
  to faith, 145
world
  hatred of, 131–33
  in rebellion against God, 134
  snares and temptations in, 135
worldliness, 134–36
worldly glory, 83
wrath of God, 56, 176

young, spiritual life of, 30

Scripture Index

Genesis
2:8 174
3:15 . . . . 54, 82, 185
3:24 175
4:4 158
17:3 180

Exodus
10:21–23 194
19 47

Numbers
14:5 180

Deuteronomy
7:6 68
18:18 52
28:22 69
28:24 69

1 Samuel
1:26 179

2 Samuel
15:23 . . . . 123, 174
15:30–31 174
15:31 123
17:1 123
17:3 123
17:23 123

Nehemiah
8:6 180

Job
1:6–12 133
2:1–6 133

Psalms
book of 34
2:7 16
2:8 110
5:11 121
6 74
6:2–5 75
6:9–10 75
8 30
8:1 54
8:2 30
17 33
17:1–3 33
17:3 34
17:15 . . . . 33, 34
22 . . . . 29, 30, 194, 197,
            200
22:1 . . . . 194, 197, 198
22:9 29
22:9–10 27
22:10 30
22:19–20 198
24:7–10 203
31 201
31:5 . . . . 201, 202
41:9 123
42:1–2 169
66:18 67
71:5–6 30

84:11 28
86:1 63
86:4 63
86:7 63
86:12–13 63
86:17 63
88 197
88:7 176
88:14 197
110:1 . . . . .120, 131, 203
116:15 164
121:1 180
142:1–4. 178
145:17. 168

Proverbs
book of 135
8:22 108
8:30–31. 127
18:10 121
28:9 67
30:7–9 136

Isaiah
1:15 68
5:13 91
6:1 138
6:3 138
6:5 96
9:6 16
11:2 40
42:1 . . . . .25, 30, 40, 138,
. . . . .155, 157
42:8 101
48:11 102
49 101
49:4 . . . . .83, 100
49:6 101
50:4 . . . . .18, 169
50:4–6. 32
50:5 182
50:5–6. 100
53 . . . . .176, 200
53:3 . . . . .62, 77, 127
53:8 197
53:10. 176
53:12. 188
54:13. 109

59:2 67
61:1 . . . . .25, 40
61:1–2. 25

Jeremiah
1:5 138
10:10. 92
31:33–34 88
32:27 87

Ezekiel
36:37 26

Daniel
2:20–21. 89
6:10 . . . . .44, 180
9 57
9:5 58

Joel
3:15 194

Amos
8:9 194

Jonah
2:3 177

Habakkuk
2:14 92

Zechariah
13:7 183

Matthew
1:18 24
1:20 24
2:1–2. 82
3:16 25
3:17 . . . . .157, 194, 195
4:3–4. 182
4:11 82
5:44 . . . . .114, 187
5:45 187
6:6 . . . . .43, 48
6:7 64
6:9 41
6:9–13. . . . . .51, 80

10:20 39
11:25 38
11:27 . . . . .39, 88, 93
12:18 25
12:28 65
13:11 110
13:35 109
14:23 . . . . .43, 46, 80
15:36 57
16:16 96
17:1 176
17:5 157
19:13 80
21:22 48
26:36 46
26:36–44 80
26:36–46 174
26:39 . . . . .39, 179
26:41 59
26:42 56
26:42–44 59
26:44 56
26:53–54 182
27:5 123
27:46 80
28:18 88
28:19–20 88

Mark
book of 44
1:15 54
1:35 . . . . .43, 44, 80
1:38 187
3:31–35 162
6:46 . . . . .43, 44, 80
8:31 77
10:45 183
13:26 165
13:32 19
14:26–41 174
14:26ff. 123
14:27–28 183
14:32–34 173
14:32–39 . . . . .44, 80
14:34 . . . . .175, 178
14:35–36 179
14:36 . . . . .42, 43, 76, 182
14:62 142

14:63–64 189
15:34 . . . . .80, 193

Luke
1:28 27
1:35 24
2 . . . . .31, 37
2:7 82
2:21 28
2:40 . . . . .31, 177
2:46–47 32
2:49 32
2:52 . . . . .32, 177
3:21 . . . . .43, 46, 80
3:21–22 62
4 25
4:1 . . . . .25, 62
4:1ff. 82
4:14 . . . . .25, 62
4:18 62
4:21 25
4:42 46
5:16 . . . . .43, 46, 80
6:12 . . . . .43, 46, 47, 80
7:44–50 82
8:21 112
9:16 57
9:18 . . . . .43, 46, 48, 80
9:20 48
9:22 48
9:28 46
9:28–29 80
9:28ff. 43
10:17 65
10:17–18 64
10:20 65
10:21 . . . . .61, 62, 63, 64, 65,
. 127
10:21–22 64
10:22 64
11:1 . . . . .52, 80
11:28 112
12:48 28
12:50 . . . . .58, 77, 176
22:17 . . . . .57, 66
22:19 57
22:31–32 133
22:39 174

22:41–45 80
22:43 184
22:44 185
22:53 81
23 187
23:21 189
23:34 . . . . .187, 188
23:43 200
23:46 . . . . 34, 37, 80, 199, 200
24:26 103

John
book of 80, 122, 126, 170
1 37
1:1 110
1:3–4 108
1:9 170
1:12–13 144
1:14 . . . . .26, 96, 110
1:18 . . . . .93, 109, 122
1:29 138
2:23–25 100
3:6–8 144
3:16 114
3:17 94
3:19–20 132
3:34 . . . . .25, 62, 138–39
3:35 87
4:34 . . . . .55, 100, 135
5:18 38
5:19 . . . . .70, 147
5:19–24 114
5:19–30 110
5:26–27 154
5:30 55
5:36 100
5:44 83
6 . . . . .56, 57
6:11 57
6:23 57
6:37 . . . . .87, 110, 163
6:38 . . . . .55, 76
6:39 . . . . .87, 163
6:45 . . . . .109, 134
6:45–46 109
6:46 110
6:57 154
6:66 101

7:6 81
7:7 . . . . .132, 134
7:8 81
7:16 170
7:18 . . . . .53, 77
7:28 168
7:30 81
8 134
8:19 168
8:20 81
8:23 134
8:24 134
8:26 170
8:29 . . . . .77, 157, 195
8:38 170
8:40 170
8:50 77
8:55 168
9:31 67
10 147
10:5–7 184
10:11 163
10:14–17 148
10:15 183
10:16 149
10:17 148
10:18 . . . . .70, 127
10:28–29 110
10:29 . . . . .87, 163
10:30 . . . . .146, 147
10:31 147
10:36 138
10:37–38 155
11 72
11:4 70
11:11 70
11:35 . . . . .70, 162
11:38–40 70
11:41–42 . . . . .67, 70, 71
11:42 72
11:50 123
12 83
12:20–21 81
12:23 81
12:27 75
12:27–28 . . . . .73, 74, 80, 81
12:31 86
12:31–32 81

12:31–33 82
12:41 138
12:43 83
12:44–45 93
12:47 114
13:1 81
13:3 87
13:10–11 123
13:12ff. 150
13:18 123
13:30 123
13:31 81
13:31–33 82
14–16 29
14:6 . . . . .16, 93, 140, 170
14:9 122
14:18–20 171
14:21–23 157
15 126
15:4–7 148
15:9–11 . . . . .126, 128
15:10 . . . . .56, 127
15:11 126
15:19–20 132
15:21 169
15:26 144
15:27 144
16:13 140
16:21 81
16:24 128
17 . . . . .53, 72, 79, 80, 93,
 101, 114, 118, 145,
 146, 149, 171
17:1 . . . . .77, 79, 84, 87
17:1–2 . . . . .85, 87
17:1–5 125
17:2 . . . . .87, 149
17:3 . . . . .86, 91, 92, 93, 94,
 111, 149, 151, 170,
 206n1 (chap. 10)
17:4 . . . . .53, 74, 77
17:4–5 99
17:5 . . . . .48, 104
17:6 . . . . .110, 121, 149, 163
17:6–8 . . . . .107, 110, 111, 122
17:7 149
17:8 . . . . .72, 110
17:9 . . . . .117, 149, 163

17:9–10 . . . . .113, 116
17:10 . . . . .84, 117, 118, 119
17:11 . . . . .119, 138, 146
17:11–12 . . . . .119, 122
17:12 123
17:13 . . . . .125, 128
17:14 131
17:14–16 . . . . .131, 135
17:15 133
17:15–16 149
17:16–17 138
17:17 . . . . .137, 140, 208n3
 (chap. 17)
17:17–19 . . . . .137, 141, 149
17:18 . . . . .94, 114
17:19 138
17:20 114
17:20–21 . . . . .143, 144
17:20–23 149
17:21 . . . . .72, 146, 149, 150
17:21–23 146
17:22 146
17:22–23 153
17:23 . . . . .146, 149, 156, 159
17:24 . . . . .103, 129, 149, 161,
 162, 165
17:25–26 167
17:26 . . . . .149, 169
18:1 . . . . .123, 174
18:6 180
18:9 175
18:11 175
20 125
20:17 41
20:21 94
21:25 97

Acts
1:9–11 120
1:11 16
2:33 144
3:17 189
7:59–60 190
10:38 . . . . .25, 135
13:27 189
13:35 201
13:52 62
20:28 . . . . .22, 116, 139, 200
26:18 . . . . .139, 144

Romans
1:4 25
2:7 83
3:21–25. 168
3:26 86
4:11 28
5:12–21. 58
8:7 131
8:9 144
8:10 155
8:11 . . . . .25, 155
8:13 . . . . .64, 139
8:15 40
8:16 40
8:18 81
8:26–27. 25
8:29 . . . . .105, 140
8:34 129
10:9 126
10:14–15 . . . . .144, 145
11:36 74
12:1–2. . . . . .133, 139
15:6–7. 117

1 Corinthians
2:8 . . . . .104, 188, 189
2:16 140
5:5 133
6:11 139
6:19–20. 139
8:6 94
10:31 . . . . .30, 74
13:4 190
13:7 190
15:15 94
15:26 162
15:27 94
15:58 55

2 Corinthians
1:20 111
2:11 133
3:18 . . . . .117, 139
4:6 86
5:7 164
5:18–19. 94
10 83

13:4 . . . . .46, 86
13:14 . . . . .74, 94

Galatians
1:4 133
2:20 129
3:16–29. 28
4:4 94
4:6 . . . . .39, 42
5:22 . . . . .62, 127, 129

Ephesians
1:3–5 114
1:4–5 105
1:5 41
1:11 182
1:13–14. 41
1:22–23. 117
1:23 74
2:4–10. 144
2:8 92
2:8–9 158
2:19 41
2:20–21. 144
3–4:16. 146
3:16 74
3:17 155
4:8 55
4:22–24. 139

Philippians
2:8 184
2:9 203
2:9–11. . . . . .84, 121
2:10–11. 96
2:11 117
2:13 155
3:10 89
4:4 . . . . .61, 128
4:5 128
4:6–7. 128
4:8–9 129

Colossians
1:15 . . . . .86, 96, 164
1:16 . . . . .56, 82
1:16–18. 74

1:27 ....129, 155, 171
2:2–3 108
2:3 ....96, 140
3:1 105

1 Thessalonians
1:6 127
1:9 92
2:13 112
4:4 139
4:13 162
4:13–17............166
5:17 31
5:18 56
5:23 ....139, 142

2 Thessalonians
2:13 139

1 Timothy
3:16 ....25, 34

2 Timothy
2:12 117
3:12 135

Titus
book of.............145
1:1–3 145

Hebrews
1:2 108
1:3 96
2:10 32
2:14 ....54, 82, 86
2:14–15.............65
4:15 ....58, 59
4:15–16.............68
5:7 ....15, 71, 120, 200
5:9 197
7:25 122
9:11–12.............122
9:14 ....25, 34, 200
10:10................139
11:6 ....43, 48
12:2 ....31, 62, 127
13:20–21 139

James
1:22 112
4:2 48
4:3 67
5:16 ....68, 71
5:17 69

1 Peter
1:7–8 117
1:19 134
2:9 68
2:21 190
3:7 67
3:13 135
3:14 135
3:16 135
3:18 ....25, 169
5:8 133

2 Peter
1:3–4 116
3:18 96

1 John
2:15 132
3:1 157
3:2 164
3:8 54
3:22 69
4:9 156
4:12 156
5:19 133

Revelation
book of.............84
1:6 117
4:8 138
5:12 84
5:12–13.............117
6:12 194
7:9 96
8:12 194
20:10................65
21:2 74
22:4 165

Also Available from Mark Jones

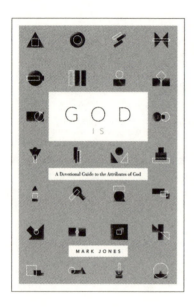

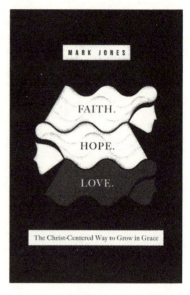

For more information, visit **crossway.org**.